SPIRITUAL EVOLUTION

SCIENTISTS DISCUSS THEIR BELIEFS

SPIRITUAL EVOLUTION

SCIENTISTS DISCUSS THEIR BELIEFS

Edited by John Marks Templeton

and Kenneth Seeman Giniger

A GINIGER BOOK

published in association with

TEMPLETON FOUNDATION PRESS
Philadelphia & London

Copyright © 1998 by The K. S. Giniger Company, Inc.

All rights reserved. No part of this publication may be reproduced, stored in a retrieval system, or transmitted in any form by any means—electronic, mechanical, photocopy, recording, or any other—except for brief quotations in printed reviews, without the prior permission of the publishers.

Requests for information should be addressed to Templeton Foundation Press, Five Radnor Corporate Center, Suite 105, 100 Matsonford Road, Radnor, Pennsylvania 19087. Published in association with The K. S. Giniger Company, Inc., 250 West 57th Street, New York, New York 10107.

Printed in the United States of America.

Library of Congress Cataloging-in-Publication Data
Spiritual evolution : scientists discuss their beliefs / edited by
    John Marks Templeton and Kenneth Seeman Giniger.
        p.   cm.
    "A Giniger book."
    "Published in association with Templeton Foundation Press."
    Includes bibliographical references.
    ISBN 1-890151-16-5
    1. Scientists—Biography.   2. Scientists—Religious life.
3. Spiritual biography.   4. Faith.   I. Templeton, John Marks, 1912–   .
II. Ginger, Kenneth Seeman, 1919–   .
Q141.S65   1998
200'.88'5—dc21   98-5985
                                                                        CIP

CONTENTS

INTRODUCTION

In planning this book, we invited a number of distinguished figures in the world of science, each known to be a believer in a Divine Being, to write about the experience or experiences that led them to this belief.

We received acceptances from figures representing such areas of scientific interest as astronomy, biology, chemistry, genetics, medicine, physics, and zoology from Australia, England, Germany, and the United States.

The standard description of arrival at believing is a dramatic one, best described in the Bible story of the conversion of Saint Paul (Acts 9:1–18; 22:1–16; 26:9–18). Paul, then known as Saul of Tarsus, was a major government persecutor of the early Christians. In the course of this task of persecution, he was on a journey to Damascus, when a light from heaven shone around him and the voice of the Lord spoke to him. This experience led to his career as the Apostle Paul.

None of the writers in this volume attest to such a "road to Damascus" experience. Their experience of belief varies, ranging from childhood influences to adult intellectual processes. And the form that belief takes also varies. Most of the writers speak of membership in mainstream Christian churches. We were, unfortunately, unable to find fundamentalist Christian or non-Christian scientists to participate, but we do not doubt that such scientists exist.

This book, then, is testimony to the fact that belief in God does not conflict with the rigid principles by which the men and women of science must test the truths of their scientific discoveries. Science and religion can and do coexist and their convergence offers mutual bene-fits.

JOHN MARKS TEMPLETON

SPIRITUAL EVOLUTION

SCIENTISTS DISCUSS THEIR BELIEFS

1

MY DAMASCUS

CHARLES BIRCH

There was a time when I thought that religious conversion was a one-off affair, as indeed it seemed to be for Saint Paul on the road to Damascus. I am not so sure now that it was even so for Saint Paul. I rather now think that I need to be converted day by day. That process had, for sure, its beginning for me, but it wasn't a once and for all phenomenon.

I was brought up as a low-church evangelical Anglican in the city of Melbourne. Sin, saving souls, a literal interpretation of the Bible, miracles, and the efficacy of the sacrament of Holy Communion were the order of the day. I accepted the lot in a formal sort of way, but the rough terrain came during adolescence. I quite suddenly came to an awareness that I was just not good enough. Even such righteousness as I might have possessed, I was reminded, was "but as filthy rags." I was quite unable to understand the powerful new urges of adolescence. I believed I must be very sinful. I read the *Confessions* of Saint Augustine and said to myself, that is I. This self-diagnosis was supported by a fundamentalist group called the Crusaders with which I got involved at Scotch College where I went to school. I never really felt at home in that group. Indeed I felt very embarrassed. I didn't want to confess my sins, whatever they were, in public and I didn't feel at home with what were called personal testimonies. I didn't have one to tell but perhaps that is what I needed. I didn't know at all what they meant by giving my life to Jesus, which they pleaded me to do. How, I asked myself, could I give myself to someone who lived two thousand years ago and whom I had never met? "Be willing to break the ice," I remember being told. I think it meant that I was to try to get over the first hurdle on the path of conversion and the rest would follow on a smoothly laid down track.

In the long hours of the night and in the early morning I pondered on all this. But all I felt was that life was a great burden and I was unable and unworthy to carry it. There was a picture in my copy of *Pilgrim's Progress* of Christian traveling on his long journey with a huge bundle on his back. Later on in the book was another picture of Christian having reached the foot of the cross and behold the bundle falls off his back to the ground. That is what I wanted to happen to me. Why didn't it? Then quite suddenly, I remember the time and the place, I asked myself, Why am I burdened with a sense of sin when Jesus says your sins are forgiven? For me that would mean that the past is the past and I could begin again right at that moment with a clean slate. I wouldn't have to carry that burden on my back anymore. So I prayed and asked for the burden to be lifted. It was. I considered myself saved.

I was by then an undergraduate at the University of Melbourne, convinced that I had the answer to life's meaning. I became a Sunday school teacher and went to evangelical meetings. My mother took me to some of them as she was a bit inclined in that direction. At least, she felt that the answers might lie there. For four undergraduate years this was my position. My classes in biology emphasized the fact of evolution but that was of little concern for me. The Bible taught otherwise and creationism was what I had to believe. I had a religious faith that encompassed the whole truth about the world. My faith was firm and my direction fixed. I wanted to convert the world. Looking back, I realize that I had not learned to think while I was an undergraduate.

Things changed when I became a graduate student at the University of Adelaide in its premier agricultural research institute. My colleagues appeared to be either atheists or agnostics. That I took religion seriously seemed very odd to them. My supervisor in particular had thought it all through and regarded religion as anti-science and a source of much evil in society. I had many discussions with him, especially when we went far into the desert on field trips. I was quite unable to defend my position intellectually. It was full of holes. My religion did not mix with my science.

Then came my second conversion. It was an intellectual conversion. The seeds of doubt had been sown and now I desperately wanted to know how to deal with them. My faith, which had given me a tremendous sense of meaning in life, was falling apart.

The beginning of a resolution to my pressing search for meaning came through the Student Christian Movement. It showed me there was an alternative interpretation of Christianity to the fundamentalism I was brought up to believe. When reassurance began to reestablish itself, it came like the weaving together of strands. I was conscious of a bottom forming under me. I tried to break it down. The strands refused to be broken. The effect was to reestablish a fundamental trust with respect to the meaningfulness of human life. I found some of the former elements came back, different from the old, no longer borrowed at second hand. For better or for worse, they were mine.

The elements of my first highly emotional conversion that came back renewed were the experiences of forgiveness, the courage to face the new, the sense of not being alone in the universe, and all that could be called the values of existence as revealed in the life of Jesus. God as the source of all value was "nearer than hands and feet, closer than breathing." The experience of God was real. The interpretation was different. This new understanding came by degrees.

I had a new problem now. The science I was becoming more familiar with presented me with a mechanistic universe, which provided no clues to the meaning of life and life's fundamental experiences of value. It had nothing to say about my feelings, which were to me the most important part of my life. How could they fit into a mechanical universe? I started on a new journey of discovery. It began when my newly found mentors in the Student Christian Movement, especially one of them, urged me to read A. N. Whitehead's *Science and the Modern World*. I felt it was written especially for me, particularly chapter five, "The Romantic Reaction." On reading Whitehead my mind flashed back to a lecture I had heard as an undergraduate, but did not understand then, by my professor of zoology, W. E. Agar. It was on the philosophy of biology. I remembered just enough about it to realize that Agar had discovered that, for him, Whitehead was fundamental to understanding philosophical problems raised by biology. So I wrote and asked him what I should now read. He replied that I should immediately read Charles Hartshorne's recently published *The Philosophy and Psychology of Sensation*. Agar added that he had himself just completed a book on a Whiteheadian interpretation of biology, modestly called *A Contribution to the Theory of the Living Organism*. Its first sentence read "The main thesis of this book is that all living organisms are subjects." That is what I needed to know. How was a biology, which looked at organisms as objects, to be reconciled with the idea of organisms as feeling subjects? I came to understand that Agar was a biologist who accepted mentality, feelings, and sentience as real and not just epiphenomena. Moreover, he identified three areas of biology that seemed resistant to a completely mechanistic analysis.

These three areas were developmental biology or embryology, behavior, and evolution. Agar was a brilliant cell biologist. He was educated at King's College, Cambridge, and at the age of thirty-eight was elected a fellow of the Royal Society. His book initiated my exploration of biology in the light of Whitehead's system of thought. Much later I was to find similar fellow feeling with the geneticist Professor C. H. Waddington, who told me on one occasion that, as an undergraduate in Cambridge, he had read all the works of Whitehead. This reading had greatly influenced both the problems he chose to work on and the manner in which he tried to solve them. As for myself I never brought all these ideas together in book form until quite recently, when I produced five books on this subject (Birch and Cobb 1981, Birch 1990, Birch 1993, Birch, Eakin and Mc Daniel 1994, Birch 1995).

As a graduate student, besides reading as much of Whitehead and Hartshorne as I could, I also read the dialogues of Plato as being highly relevant, and on more specifically religious topics I read as much of Harry Emerson Fosdick as I could lay my hands on. He was at that time the pastor of the great interdenominational, interracial, and international Riverside Church in New York, hard by Columbia University. He was a great preacher and had an evangelical liberal theology that had got him into trouble with the General Assembly of the

Presbyterian Church in the United States when he was pastor of Manhattan's First Presbyterian Church. He was charged with heresy but responded that he would be ashamed to live in this generation and not be a heretic. This was the time, said Reinhold Niebuhr, in which the old evangelical piety of American Protestantism, so vital in its earlier form and so potent in taming an advancing frontier, had hardened into a graceless biblicism and legalism.

Fosdick had fought his way through the fundamentalism of his youth to a rational faith. Many a student, in particular, had his faith restored and saved by this great preacher so far ahead of his time. From time to time I still refer to one or other of his many published sermons and I always try to make a pilgrimage to Riverside Church when in New York. On the first visit I made in 1946 (the year of Fosdick's retirement), I was able to tell Fosdick what an influence he had been to me and other students I knew in Australia. So I am delighted that one of his hymns "God of grace and God of glory" is included in *The Australian Hymn Book*. It was written for the dedication of Riverside Church in 1931:

> Set our feet on lofty places;
> gird our lives that they may be
> armoured with all Christ-like graces
> in the fight to set men free.
> Grant us wisdom,
> grant us courage,
> that we fail not man nor thee.

In the 1950s when I was doing research at Columbia University, I became a member of Riverside Church. Later, as a link with Australia, I presented to the chapel of Wesley College in the University of Sydney a set of silver plated individual communion chalices identical with those used at Riverside Church.

An account of my journey as a graduate student would not be complete without indicating how important it was for me at this stage to have the friendship of those who had gone further on the journey than I had. In particular there was one senior person in the Student Christian Movement in the University of Adelaide. He was then a lecturer in philosophy. Toward the end of my time as a graduate student in Adelaide I wrote about him in the national journal of the SCM without mentioning either my name or his. I called my contribution "Somebody." It read in part as follows:

> I had just graduated at the University. It was a strange feeling, I was supposed to know so much, yet was inwardly conscious that life was a mystery to me. There were threads of meaning in parts, but they became tangled once I tried to follow their course, and try I did—desperately. There were things about God I felt I ought to believe, but I didn't know why. Some of my colleagues called them fantasies of the imagination. I began to wonder myself. At times I would have thrown religion overboard, partly for moral and partly for intellectual reasons. Yet I shrank from the prospect of a youth bereft of idealism. Then things changed. That was when somebody came. He had strong convictions about Jesus and God. The threads in his life were not tangled. I know now why mine were, they were a mixture of false and true strands. I didn't know that then—not until he came. There was something compelling about his convictions. In the friendship that followed he didn't teach me so much as show me where to discover God. He led me to still waters. He was helping me to do what I never thought I could do before. He was what Emerson said of a friend, "what we need is somebody who will help us to do what we can." I see now that he believed in me when I didn't believe in myself. His was a faith in the infinite possibilities God's universe holds for human beings and a faith in the capacity of each of us to respond.
>
> He was a missionary, not the sort who goes to foreign countries but one in our midst. I came to the conviction that the greatest service we can render anyone is to show that person what he or she can be. On the highways and byways of Palestine, Jesus of Nazareth was that Somebody to everyone who needed him; to the woman at the well in Samaria, to Zacchaeus up a tree, to Peter and James and John by their nets. In the last hour that life held for him, despite the agony of the cross, he was that Somebody to a wretched thief on a cross beside him. There is an old evangelical hymn that begins, "Somebody came," and then asks, "Was that somebody you?"

My new discoveries of the meaning of my life led me to be dissatisfied with the prospect of a career devoted entirely to research. I loved research and the research institute in which I was working, but I wanted also to be more involved with people. The obvious way to do that was to combine research with teaching. I felt I needed experience in a teaching and research department. I can even now vividly recall the exact spot on the winding road going up the foothills behind Adelaide when I made a decision. I was riding on my bicycle and stopped for a break. Stretching out below me were the extensive grounds and buildings of the Waite Agricultural Research Institute. They symbolized full time research for me. That was great, but not enough. Moreover, I was fast becoming more inclined to fundamental problems in biology instead of applied agricultural ones, which had involved me thus far. On that spot I made a decision to seek further experience in a biology department overseas.

The obvious place for population biology in the late 1940s was the University of Chicago. Furthermore, I had a lurking feeling that perhaps I had got myself on a false path about life's meaning. I had done that once before with fundamentalism. In Adelaide I was antipodes away from the process thought of Whitehead. I needed to test out my convictions in a completely different environment. To Chicago I went.

Unknown to me, when I set out for the University of Chicago to do research and sit in on biology courses, that university was, at that time, the world center of process (Whiteheadian) thought. Professor Charles Hartshorne was in the department of philosophy. In the Divinity School were professors Henry Nelson Wieman, Bernard Meland, Bernard Loomer, and Daniel Day Williams. To add yet more to these riches, the most distinguished professor in the department of zoology, where I was to be, was Sewall Wright. Not only was he one of the four founding fathers of the neo-Darwinian synthesis of evolution (the others being Sir Ronald Fisher, J. B. S. Haldane, and Theodosius Dobzhansky), he was also a Whiteheadian and close friend of Charles Hartshorne. Some years later in 1953 Wright gave the presidential address entitled "Gene and Organism" to the American Society of Naturalists. It was a closely argued case for the gene as an organism and therefore a subject and not a mere object.

My days in Chicago were spent in the laboratory interspersed by sitting in on courses on evolution, genetics, ecology, and process theology. I learned a great deal about university education of a sort I had never known before. Robert Maynard Hutchins was the brilliant young chancellor of the university who, through his unusual vision, was transforming the University of Chicago. He said he wanted a football team that was proud of the university, not the other way around.

These were heady days. My new experiences were reinforcing the foundations of my thinking. I knew I was on a road I would not now leave. While I was at the University of Chicago, I got to know Ian Barbour who was then completing his Ph.D. in physics and who later was to become a world leader in the relation of science and religion. Over the years we have had many discussions on this subject. Early on he gave me reinforcement as a physicist who was reconciling physics and religion while I was trying to do the same with biology.

I came to know Charles Hartshorne and his wife Dorothy in subsequent years both on his visits to Australia and on mine to the United States. One day I asked him whom else I should get to know. He immediately replied, "My most brilliant student, John Cobb." So began a friendship with John Cobb, of the Center for Process Studies at Claremont, California, which led us to work together on process thought and biology. Our work led to a consultation at the Rockefeller Center for Consultations at Villa Serbelloni in Bellagi, Italy in 1974 and a book *Mind in Nature* (eds. John B. Cobb and David Ray Griffin). Later Cobb and I wrote together *The Liberation of Life: From the Cell to the Community.*

In my years overseas I remained involved in the Student Christian Movement as part of the World Student Christian Federation. My first truly ecumenical experience was as one of the representatives of the Australian SCM at the first world conference of Christian Youth in Oslo in 1947. After that meeting I went on to spend a week at a chalet in Grindelwald, Switzerland with a group of European students who had suffered grievously in the war. My roommate was a German student who had been captured by Australians when serving in the German Army in North Africa! I realized how terrible war is—a few years earlier I would have been required to regard him as an enemy. From that moment on, I felt a certain empathy with German students, an empathy that was to develop when my involvement with the World Council of Churches brought me into various parts of East Germany.

Thanks in part to the Australian Student Christian Movement, I was for twenty years a member of the working committee of the World Council of Churches that dealt with science, environment, and technology. During this part of my life the World Council of Churches was virtually staffed by former students of the Student Christian Movement. The SCMs throughout the world were a sort of a training ground for the world ecumenical movement. We seemed to know one another. Most of my involvement with the WCC was with staff member Dr. Paul Abrecht. He had come from Union Theological Seminary in New York in the great days of Reinhold Niebuhr. His influence prevented me from running away with too utopian visions, and to recognize the ambiguities in almost everything we do.

My researches in the ecological aspects of evolution brought me to work in the laboratory of Theodosius Dobzhansky, first at Columbia University in New York, later in Brazil, and still later when he came to work in my laboratory at the University of Sydney.

Dobzhansky was a challenge to my thinking. He was a strict Darwinian and famous as such. But all the time lurking in the back of his mind was his upbringing in Russia in the Orthodox Church. How could he link the two? That was a problem for him when we first met. He was not enthusiastic about the synthesis of science and religion, which I was discovering through A. N. Whitehead's thought. He was more interested in the synthesis of Teilhard de Chardin, who was both palaeontologist and priest. He was drawn to the Omega notion of Teilhard that there was a final goal to which cosmic evolution moved. However, he rejected Teilhard's central tenet (which is also Whitehead's) of a "within of things." This is the notion that every individual entity, from quarks to humans, has a subjective aspect, which in humans is manifested as consciousness.

I persuaded Dobzhansky to come with me to some lectures by Paul Tillich. He immediately became attracted to Tillich's concept of "ultimate concern," which is essentially Tillich's synonym for the word God. How, Dobzhansky asked, could human concern for ultimate concern have evolved? This pursuit resulted in his book *The Biology of Ultimate Concern*. Dobzhansky was struggling, as was I, with the problem of the evolution of the subjective. My Whiteheadian solution was that the subjective in some form existed all the way from quarks to people. Dobzhansky argued that the subjective (such as mentality) emerged at some stage in the evolution of animals. We ever remained to differ on this subject, as is evident in his later book *The Biological Basis of Human Freedom*. But my many discussions with Dobzhansky, both in the laboratory and in the jungles of Brazil and Australia, helped me to see the central importance of the issue. Neither Dobzhansky nor I had much support from the leading evolutionists of the day, such as Ernst Mayr and G. G. Simpson, who were his close friends and strict mechanists in their thinking. They inclined to blame me for leading Dobzhansky astray from the strictly mechanistic path.

The evolution of mentality, or as I prefer to call it, the subjective, is precisely the problem Whitehead (1933) had laid out clearly when he wrote:

> A thoroughgoing evolutionary philosophy is inconsistent with material-ism. The aboriginal stuff, or material, from which a materialistic philos-ophy starts is incapable of evolution. This material is in itself the ultimate substance. Evolution, on the materialistic theory, is reduced to the role of being another word for the description of the changes of the external relations between portions of matter. There is nothing to evolve, because one set of external relations is as good as any other set of external relations. There can be merely change, purposeless and unpro-gressive. . . . The doctrine thus cries aloud for a conception of organism as fundamental for nature (p. 134).

The conception of organism, which Whitehead called the philoso-phy of organism, involves a radical departure from the interpretation of living organism as machine. It is the principle that sees human experi-ence as a high-level exemplification of reality in general. All individual entities from quarks to people are understood to be constituted by something analogous to experience as we know it in our own lives and which, for want of another term, is called experience. Hence an alter-native name for Whitehead's philosophy of organism is the philosophy of panexperientalism. It involves the proposition that mentality cannot arise from no-mentality. Subjectivity cannot emerge from something that is not subjective. Freedom and self-determination cannot arise from something completely devoid of freedom and self-determination. Instead of sentience or experience being a late arrival in the evolution of the cosmos it is there from the first entities of the creation. All individual entities from quarks to people have in common with human experience that they take account of their environment through their internal relations. Most western thought has focused on external relations (that push or pull). An external relation does not affect the nature of the things related. An internal relation is different. It is constitutive of the character and even the existence of something. As Tennyson put into the mouth of the adventurous Ulysses, "I am a part of all that I have met."

The principle of panexperientalism is implicit in the rhetorical question of quantum physicist J. A. Wheeler, who asked, "Here is a man so what must the universe be?" We cannot know what the universe is in its fundamental nature unless we take account of the experiencing human being who evolved within it. From a universe which at its early stage consisted of hydrogen there evolved complex molecules and eventually humans. These and everything in between were potentialities from the foundation of the universe.

Where then does the concept of God fit into this scenario? In my earlier unenlightened days I had imagined God as a divine engineer who manufactured things much as a watchmaker might make a watch. But Darwin showed that concept just did not square with what he was discovering in the theory of natural selection of chance variations. Darwinism was a mortal blow to the natural theology of his day. It did not of course rule out the possibility of another concept of God. My next step with Whitehead moved in that direction.

In contemplating the cosmic evolutionary process Whitehead argued that "the potentiality of the universe must be somewhere." By "somewhere," he meant "some actual entity." He named that actual entity the mind of God. More importantly the nature of divine activity in the universe is that of loving persuasion. I became very aware that the concepts of divine omnipotence and ruler are no longer applicable, but that persuasive love is the only power that matters. I was brought back to the image of Jesus as the meaning of love in human life and that same love as a divine influence in the whole universe. God acts by being felt by his creatures, be those creatures protons or people. God as persuasive love is ever confronting the world with the possibilities of its future.

This became a very personalistic view of God for I was able to recognize that the God who influenced human life was at work in the same way in the rest of the creation. I was finding a new meaning for divine purpose. Previously I had thought in terms of the design image. But the potentialities of the universe and the way they are realized are not in the form of a blueprint for the future. I came to see that it was misleading to speak of a divine design. The term design connotes a preconceived detailed plan, which is one reason why Darwinism dealt such a severe blow to the deism of William Paley's *Natural Theology*, which Darwin had read as a student at Cambridge. The term purpose is better than design as it does not carry this connotation. Nothing is completely determined. I learned that from science. The future is open-ended. I came to see that one reason why this is so is that God is not the sole cause of all happenings. God exercises causality always in relation to beings who have their own measure of self-determination. God is our companion in the creative advance toward the realization of as yet unrealized possibilities. "In every event," said Martin Buber, "we are addressed by God." So it is of the rest of the creation.

All this led me to a new understanding of the meaning of providence. Providence is a difficult word with a number of meanings. It does not mean a divine planning in which everything is predetermined, as in the making of a machine. Rather it means that there is a creative and saving possibility in every situation which cannot be destroyed by any event. The form of power that is most admirable and creative is not a coercive power but one that empathizes with others and empowers them.

It is true that some events in the history of the cosmos, including human history, have more significance than others. These are peak events. I used to think of them as special acts of the power of God intervening in a special way in the world. I now see that that way of looking at peak events turns God into an agent of mechanical intervention, even into a magician. It replaces persuasive love with fiat.

But what of the evil in the world? I never found credible the notion that all was created perfect until humans entered the picture and then all went awry. Yet evil, both in nature and in human life, is a reality. I came to see that if God is understood as that factor in the universe that makes for novelty, life, intensity of feeling, consciousness, and freedom, we must recognize that God is also responsible for the evil in the world. If there were nothing at all or total chaos, or if there were only some very simple levels of order, there would be little evil. There would instead be the absence of both good and evil. Earthquakes and tornadoes would be neither good nor evil in a world devoid of life. Only where there are significant values does the possibility of their thwarting and their destruction arise. The possibility of pain is the price paid for consciousness and the capacity for intense feeling. Evil exists as the corruption of the capacity for love. Thus God, by creating good, provides the context within which there is evil. In this view evil springs not from providence but from chance and freedom, without which there could not be a world.

I learned from Paul Tillich, both in his classes in New York and from his sermons, that our only adequate response to God's persuasive love, the love of ultimate concern, is infinite passion. This is the "with all" of which Jesus speaks. We are called to total response of heart and mind and strength. It seems to me in looking back that my evangelical beginning taught me the response of the heart but it let me down in an adequate response of the mind. The Student Christian Movement taught me the meaning of giving an intellectual account for what I believed. It is as though I experienced God first and spent the rest of my life seeking to explain what I had experienced. And the more I understood the more I was able to experience. That brings a vividness to human experience as expressed by T. S. Eliot:

> We had the experience but missed the
> meaning.
> And approach to the meaning restores the
> experience.
> In different form.

Yet the heavenly city of Enlightenment has not arrived. I learned from Reinhold Niebuhr that the will to live truly is readily transmuted in human lives into the will to power. The will to live truly is transmuted by overweening self-interest into a will to power that is destructive. The same person who has the capacity for transcending self-interest also reveals varying degrees of the power of self-interest and the subservience of the will to those interests. I now know that conversion is not a once and for all phenomenon. I need to be reborn day by day, hour by hour, for self-interest is not annihilated once and for all time. I think that is because there is a valid side to self-interest that can be creative. When I give a lecture I want it to influence my audience. To do so, I need to put on a dramatic performance. I then become important; indeed, the lecture is not likely to be much good unless I also receive satisfaction from it. I get satisfaction from the response of the audience but I should not let my satisfaction become excessive. I need to be eternally vigilant if I am not to fall over backwards on this knife-edge of life.

If we are co-creators with God, it is important for me to know if our contribution is lasting or if it fades with death. The question is relevant not just in relation to my death but to the ultimate death of the universe as understood by cosmologists. I have never been able to accept the notion of human purpose if there is not some cosmic purpose to which human purpose contributes. Yet I never found the notion of postmortem rewards and punishments at all appealing. What I eventually did find helpful was Whitehead's proposition that it is as true to say that the world experiences God as the world is created as to say that God experiences the world as the world is created—that everything we do and everything every creature does makes a difference to God. The universe would never be as it is if we had never been! God is both cause in creating the world and effect in experiencing the world. There is biblical testimony to a God who is deeply involved with his creation and with its joys and suffering. God is not the producer of the play who stands in the wings watching the performance. God is on stage feeling every feeling with utter intensity (Rom. 8). So in this sense God saves the world as it is created and every creation becomes a novel experience for God. This is the most speculative part of Whitehead's thought about God. Like other intellectual constructions about God, it is to varying degrees provisional in character. Subscription to creeds is a danger to the integrity of conscience. Yet there remains the necessity of some meaning of a cosmic purpose that transcends the world and all its experiences as it is created. Some doctrine of immortality is needed in a purposive cosmos. Many churches put this in terms of affirmations of detailed belief. For me it is not belief but faith.

The essence of Christianity for me is incarnate in the person and teaching of Jesus. It is faith in God as ultimate concern. It is faith in the divinity of men and women revealed in Jesus. It is faith in the possibilities and sacredness of human life and in the life of all creatures. I feel called to respond to ultimate concern with all my heart and mind and strength. So I have increasingly felt across the years the necessity of being able to give an intellectual as well as an experiential account of my faith.

References

Agar, W. E. *A Contribution to the Theory of the Living Organism.* Melbourne: Melbourne University Press and Oxford University Press, 1943.

Birch, Charles. *On Purpose.* Kensington: New South Wales University Press, 1990. Also published as *A Purpose for Everything.* Mystic, Conn.: Twenty-Third Publications, 1990.

————. *Regaining Compassion: For Humanity and Nature.* St. Louis, Mo.: Chalice Press, 1993.

————. *Feelings.* Kensington: New South Wales University Press, 1995.

Birch, Charles and John B. Cobb. *The Liberation of Life: From the Cell to the Community.* Cambridge: Cambridge University Press, 1981.

Birch, Charles, William Eakin, and Jay B. McDaniel. *Liberating Life: Contemporary Approaches to Ecological Theology.* Maryknoll, N.Y.: Orbis Books, 1994.

Dobzhansky, Theodosius. *The Biology of Ultimate Concern.* New York: New American Library, 1967.

————. *The Biological Basis of Human Freedom.* New York: Columbia University Press, 1956.

Hartshorne, Charles. *The Philosophy and Psychology of Sensation.* Chicago: University of Chicago Press, 1934.

Whitehead, A. N. *Science and the Modern World.* Cambridge: Cambridge University Press, 1933.

Wright, Sewall. "Gene and Organism." *American Naturalist* 87 (1953): 5–18.

2

QUIET PATH,

QUIET POOL

S. JOCELYN BELL BURNELL

I was born and brought up a Quaker, a member of the Religious Society of Friends, and continue in that tradition as an active member. Since readers may be unfamiliar with British Quakerism, this essay will start with some explanation of that tradition.

What Is Quakerism?

Quakerism in the United States is particularly diverse, containing within the one nation the full range of possible theologies and practices. It stretches from evangelical through conservative to liberal. Some still wear the special dress and a few still address one another as "thee" and "thou." Many congregations have pastors and choirs and a set form of service not very different from other reformed Protestant denominations. Many carry out evangelical missionary work in Africa or Latin America.

There are many also that still have the unprogramed Meetings for Worship, where the congregation gathers in silence quietly worshiping and waiting. Out of the silence, words may be spoken in ministry by anyone present—there is no designated minister. It is held that there is that of God (sometimes called the Inner Light) in everyone, and that everyone can have direct access to God, no intermediary being necessary.

It is to this latter style of Quakerism that I belong and so it seems appropriate to say rather more about it. Peace, justice, reconciliation, and the relief of suffering have long been Quaker concerns. There are testimonies also to simplicity (of lifestyle) and truthfulness. Quaker burial grounds are recognizable by the uniform and plain style of head-stone—a manifestation of our belief that all are equal in the sight of God. For this reason, too, titles are not used and we know each other simply by our first name and family name, not as Mr. or Lady or (even) Professor. Special times, or holy days, were also frowned upon as it was felt that the sacred could not and should not be confined to certain oc-casions. We are more relaxed now and celebrate birthdays, Christmas, and so on, but we are aware that even in our daily lives we can be walk-ing on holy ground, and encountering God in other people.

There are three possible sources of authority for a faith or denomi-nation. These are a) its holy writings, b) its history and tradition, and c) ongoing revelation. Quakerism is unusual in that it gives greatest weight to this last source, the continuing revelation of God and God's will for the community. We place less weight upon the Bible than do the other Christian denominations, and this causes considerable confu-sion. The real touchstone, for us, is what we believe to be the leading of God (through the Holy Spirit) given to us in our generation. A lot of our practice is directed toward correctly discerning those leadings and not being misled by bees in the private bonnets of articulate members. We have a strong tradition of testing leadings in the community by the community. (There is also the converse of this, when the community identifies an individual as a suitable person for a particular task. In-spired nominations committees have rightly suggested people for roles that they had never dreamt of assuming.) The emphasis on continuing revelation and on our experience of God in our lives today is important for scientists, and we will return to this matter shortly.

Quaker Women

One of the basic tenets of Quakerism is that the Holy Spirit can, and does, work through anyone, woman, man, or child. For generations the equality of Quaker women has been recognized (in theory at least). Quaker women are used to contributing in decision-making and are used to being heard. I notice that in ecumenical discussions I am more confident about speaking out than are many women from male-dominated denominations. Having said that, it must be acknowledged that Quakers are inevitably influenced by the society in which we live and one finds that the catering committee, the children's class committee, and the group charged with pastoral care are predominantly female, while the finance and property committee is largely male! Nonetheless, the fact that I am a Quaker woman has doubtless colored my attitude to life. Those who know me better than I know myself say it explains a lot!

Experience and Experiment

The emphasis placed by Quakerism on continuing revelation means that nothing is fixed, nothing is static. Every twenty-five or thirty years we completely revise our books of faith and discipline, re-forming our sense of who we are, articulating our faith in contemporary language, and restating our procedural regulations. (Quakers in Britain last did this in 1994, and their subsequent book *Quaker Faith and Practice* is recommended to those who would like to know more about Quakerism. Other Quaker groupings have similar publications.) We have no creed that members are expected to subscribe to, partly because we have seen how our understanding can change, partly because words can change their meaning, and mean different things to different people, but largely because we believe we are dealing with something beyond words. Nevertheless, there is a clear body of Quaker belief, and there is an even clearer body of attitude and action arising from that belief. One of the things that holds us together is a sense of seeking and exploring, and arguably it is this that has made the Religious Society of Friends so acceptable to so many scientists. John Dalton (of atomic fame), Arthur Stanley Eddington (the astrophysicist) and Kathleen Lonsdale (the crystallographer) are some of the best-known Quaker scientists. There are others living now that I will not embarrass by mentioning here. The scientist works by experimenting, noting the outcome of the experiment, reformulating her or his understanding in the light of that outcome, devising further experiments, and repeating the cycle. In an analogous way Quakers gain experience of God's working in the world, revise their understanding in the light of that experience, and look to see what is required of them next. From time to time scientists meet dead ends in their research and to make further progress have to back out and come at the problem from a different angle. Problems are usually resolved by approaches from several angles; each approach contributes, and the solution is often found to be something larger than any one approach. Similarly, as our understanding of God grows it can be appreciated that another's experience is complementary, that no one possesses the Ultimate truth, and that the Ultimate truth is probably beyond literal expression. Both the scientist and the religious person must respect the outcome of the experiment/experience, not trying to force it into a familiar, comfortable mould, but being prepared for a drastic revision, if that is what the data dictates. There are clear parallels in the ways the two disciplines work.

One Scientist's Path

As a teenager I looked for proof of the existence of God, but soon realized there would be none. So I chose to adopt, as a working hypothesis, a belief in God, and to go on from there. Now, forty years later, I remain tentative, but more sure than I was as a teenager. My path is best described as a process of evolving understanding rather than one punctuated by events that have revolutionized my thinking. Sometimes the process has moved ahead smoothly, sometimes it has barely moved, but gradually experience has convinced me of the existence of God. It is very personal (idiosyncratic), and doubtless it would not convince anyone else, but it has allowed me to shift the balance of my opinion. The primary experience comes through the Quaker Meeting for Worship. Description of that is deferred till later because it reveals much else besides. The other powerful learning experience has been the result of being asked by Quakers to do things that I was not sure I had the ability to do. It is part of the discipline to respect the wisdom of a Quaker search group, and so I found myself accepting, but quite unclear how I was going to carry out these, invariably very public, tasks. Thinking hard, praying hard, and listening to my own inner wisdom resulted in a sense of being held, supported, and gently prodded in certain directions. The struggle to articulate afresh and find the right words is part of the growth—now as then!

Of course, there have also been bad times. Death, disease, divorce, and disappointment have all visited me. They too provide learning experiences, and are not to be brushed aside abruptly, but are to be worked with and used. (This was a topic that I addressed in greater detail in a lecture and book that Quakers asked me to prepare, *Broken for Life.*) I have had to develop techniques for holding on, hanging in there. The Quaker Meeting for Worship provides few props and there have been times when the only thing I could do was attend Meeting for Worship as a "passenger." My discipleship could extend to that, but no further. Probably we all have times when we need others to make our communion for us—perhaps that is what communities are for! Another hazard, possibly peculiar to Quakerism, is being too rushed, too stressed, with insufficient space or relaxation to allow one to center down into worship. Will rampant competitiveness, which seems to be the ethos in the United Kingdom at the moment, leave us so harassed that this lack of space becomes a problem? Practice makes perfect, so they say. It has certainly been my experience that when I can give more time, more regularly to silent worship and to consideration of things spiritual, the more deeply, more readily I can engage. Working in the spirit like this provides a real sense of quiet joy, and a wish for further engagement.

We articulate and explain our innermost experiences in a framework and language. Mine happens to be broadly Christian because Christianity is where I started, by accident of birth. Furthermore it is western European Christianity, because that was the culture in which I grew up. Much Christian language makes me blink a bit, but I have learned that behind some of this peculiar vocabulary there are profound and valuable truths. That is not to say that I accept *all* the Christian tradition unquestioningly.

Traditional Quaker wisdom includes the advice to be open to fresh light from whatever quarter it may come. Quakers have an open, respectful attitude towards other faiths—we are not aggressively Christian. Some of us have found it helpful to include elements from other world faiths in our personal theologies. I find myself absorbed in

Christianity, still digging into it, still trying to plumb its depths. I suspect I have more than a lifetime's work there!

Rational Belief

Belief structures are affairs of the head as well as the heart, and should ideally also satisfy our rational beings. However, this is an area where there is considerable danger—danger caused by the human desire to have a neat, preferably watertight, package. This may not be possible. Even if it is possible, the package may not be the one we wanted. Are we prepared for this? Is there a desire to make the data confirm our previous picture of God? Rather than forcing data, I prefer to say that I do not know the answers to a number of questions. Being able to say "don't know" requires an ability to live with unresolved issues, which is a form of maturity. Perhaps because I study a dynamic cosmos, which has an inherent uncertainty (namely Heisenberg's Uncertainty Principle), I am reasonably comfortable with change and lack of certainty, with moving on, and with accepting that one does not understand it all.

I believe in a God who is (can be) powerful and all-knowing, but also caring and forgiving. This combination runs us promptly into the problem of suffering. There is an amazing variety of "explanations" for suffering, none of which seems completely logical to me. (Again, see my book for more details.) It does show how much we want explanations, however. I am loath to abandon the idea of a caring God, but do toy with the idea that God may not be directly running the world, but only indirectly, through people.

Science and Belief

There is, reportedly, a tension between science and religion. I am unclear what the problem is, but clearly some church members feel this is an area of difficulty. Scientists, by and large, are unconcerned probably because they feel religion is unimportant and not worth worrying about. Perhaps it is because my denomination allows me to draw my own boundaries that I have not hit "the problem." I do not have to believe literally in the story of the creation in Genesis (either version); I do not have to believe in a creator God. I do not have to believe in original sin, miracles, tangible resurrections from the dead, and so on. Our approach is rather more, "Well, what can you believe?" It is a relatively baggage-free approach. Perhaps it is also a light-weight approach.

There is a problem associated with the use of images. I was surprised when a Soviet Minister of State said to us, a delegation from the British churches, "We know there is no God. We have sent satellites up into space, and God is not to be found there." I had not appreciated that some people take (or choose to take) the "old man in the sky" image so literally. There can be similar problems to do with the way religion is taught to children. In adulthood people discover that the childish imagery presented to them is not literally true, and abandon the whole lot as untrue.

It appears to me as an astronomer that the universe evolved by itself, without the active participation of God. True, there is a tiny fraction of a second close to the initial Big Bang that scientists cannot address, and there are those who say that in this tiny fraction of a second God "lit the blue touchpaper." This argument is poor a) because it is too like the "God-of-the-gaps" theology with its obvious limitations, and b) because it smacks of wishful thinking. I prefer to say that I am not sure that God was the creator of the universe, in the literal sense, but nonetheless I am sure there is a God with relevance to us today, regardless of what (s)he did or did not do fifteen billion years ago.

Life can only exist in the universe if the values of a number of physical constants are simultaneously set within narrow bands. There seems to be no reason why the constants should all take those particular values, and some will argue from this that therefore there must be a God who set it all up so that the universe was suitable for life (as we know it). This feels to me like a theology desperately searching for proof! We only know about a small fraction of the universe and have no guarantee that the other bits are like this bit. For all we know there may be other versions that are totally different.

The universe we already know about is vast, with huge numbers of stars. Many of these will be stars like our sun, and some will have habitable planets. Are we alone in the universe or is there (has there been, will there be) life elsewhere? My theology has to take account of the fact that we are probably not unique, and we are probably not alone (but the chances of intervisitation are small). One wonders whether they too needed a Jesus Christ.

Another thought-provoking issue concerns the nature of hope and the future of the universe. Even if humankind avoids self-destruction the outlook is bleak. The sun, on which we are heavily dependent for life, will one day die. The earth will die with it. Perhaps we will take to our spaceships and move elsewhere, but there is no long-term escape. There seem to be three possible outcomes for the future of the universe (cosmologists are not yet clear which will actually happen)—and all of them are fatal for life. What gospel do we preach in the face of this?

Head Work and Heart Work

This is heady stuff, and intellectually stimulating! It gives us a sense of long sight, of overview, and a seductive detachment from everyday living. But what are we overlooking? We are not Lords of the Universe. We are not omnipotent. We are not (by and large) in control of our lives. Focusing on plans and goals is properly a part of our lives, but is wrong if it causes us to neglect the here and now, the process of being, the faithful living.

In a society that applauds vigor and success it is tempting to dismiss all thought of weakness and failure. However, we diminish our living unless we recognize our limitations; we may become wounded healers if we can accept them. I have come to recognize the special ministry of the disabled, the hurt, the wounded, to recognize the power in powerlessness and the strength in vulnerability. In a sense we are all disabled, hurt, and wounded, vulnerable and powerless, and we are glorious because of these.

In the Quaker Meeting for Worship

The form of Quaker Meeting for Worship that I am used to is a community gathered in expectant silence, open, faithfully waiting for the "promptings of love and truth" which are felt to be the leadings of

God. It doesn't happen every time, but there can be profound moments in a Meeting for Worship when the meeting collectively becomes deep, gathered, still. The presence of God may be so strongly felt that breathing is prayer and worship and communion. At such times I feel an assurance, affirmed and empowered. I can be myself, accept myself, and drop all masks. It comes naturally to be quiet, yet full of wordless praise, to acknowledge God as holy and as Lord (whatever those words mean—the words I really want aren't in my vocabulary, indeed maybe do not exist). Some of us can have the same sense outside Meeting for Worship. There is a timelessness about it. There is also a realization that questions which only an hour ago seemed very important (e.g., was God the creator of the universe?) drop away as irrelevant. This present, this presence is the reality. It is a yearning for this sense of communion that keeps me going, and keeps me going to Quaker meeting.

References

Quaker Faith and Practice: the Book of Christian Discipline of the Religious Society of Friends (Quakers) in Britain. Britain Yearly Meeting, 1995.

Burnell, S. Jocelyn Bell. *Broken for Life.* London: Quaker Home Service, 1989.

3

TRACKS IN SNOW

LARRY DOSSEY

The traces of one's life disappear quickly, like tracks in snow. It is good that they do. Otherwise the human landscape would be horribly cluttered, and those who come after us would be confused by the aimless meanderings of those who have come before.

Because it is difficult to see the tracks we have left, it is impossible to cobble together the events in our lives that have led to our present place. Again, this is not all bad; our faulty memories unburden us from the past and help us rest in the present.

I have a resistance to reflecting on my "path." The slightest reflection shows that our life's path is rarely straight, purposeful, or efficient. Speaking of one's "journey" is a bit contrived, because this suggests that we have always known where we were going. So although I shall describe some of the events of my journey and the conclusions to which they have led, I hope you will bear in mind that my path is one which I usually have not seen clearly at the time.

My current spiritual views have largely resulted from a collision in my life between science and religion. These terrible struggles have caused me immense unhappiness for long periods, but they have eventually led, mercifully, to a deep sense of serenity and peace. Joseph Campbell, the great mythologist, once said that we acquire wisdom through two ways, revelation and suffering. One can experience a sudden epiphany—Saul on the road to Damascus, Bernadette at the grotto, the Buddha during meditation—but these are not as frequent as we wish. "It is no good angling for the rich moments," C. S. Lewis once said. In contrast, opportunities to gain wisdom through suffering are abundant!

I grew up in a deeply religious culture, the cotton-farming prairies of central Texas. We regarded ourselves as inhabitants of not just the Bible Belt but of the *buckle* of the Bible Belt. Growing up, fundamentalist Christianity was my religious sustenance which, of course, I never questioned as a child. The church was the social institution around which rural society orbited, and I was caught up in it. I was musically gifted and played the piano for church, for a professional gospel quartet, and occasionally for a roving, fiery tent evangelist.

As a child, I thought I would become a minister, but as it came time for college, I chose to enter the University of Texas at Austin and pursue a career in science. I fell in love with biology, chemistry, physiology, pharmacology. I obtained a degree in pharmacy and followed a "pre-med" program in preparation for medical school.

It is difficult to describe my early fascination with empiricism. It was as if whole areas of my mind were opened up for the first time. Years later I encountered a description of these experiences that rang true. Jacob Needleman, the philosopher of religion, in his book, *A Sense of the Cosmos*, described the motivations and feelings of the first scientists.[1] In his graphic metaphor, he stated that they went to "the wall of truth" in search of an *unmediated confrontation with reality.* They did so in protest of the church, which at that time defined the world for everyone. This motivation, said Needleman, is the ancient mystical urge, the desire personally and intimately to know the Absolute without the interference or interpretation of anyone else. This described my own encounter with science: a mystical, life-changing event. Yet immense difficulties began to arise. The scientific picture of the world presented by the academicians was aridly materialistic. The world, I learned, was on automatic, under the grip of the so-called ironclad laws of nature. There was no place whatever in this construction for values or goals. To propose that the world was guided by purpose was to betray science and reason. This picture was spartan and uncompromising; any other option was an indication of intellectual softheadedness.

Consequently, I, like thousands of young people before and after me, perceived that there were two ways of ordering one's life. One could choose, on the one hand, to be rational, analytical, logical, and scientific. Or one could choose to be intuitive, religious, spiritual, and intellectually reckless. It was obvious to me that these two psychological vectors—science and "the spiritual"—were inherently incompatible and could not be harmonized.

Although today I regard these choices as artificial, at the time they seemed valid and ineluctable. They persist in our colleges and universities. These choices are, literally, schizophrenic because they create a false division in the mind. These false choices have caused immense pain for millions of questing, bright young people, because they require a bifurcated existence that is unnatural and that feels deeply wrong.

When religion and scientific materialism collide, it is usually religion that gets the worst of it. So it was in my experience. I set aside my previous religious leanings and became thoroughly agnostic. At the time, I mistook the enthusiasm of the scientists who were my teachers for reason. I assumed their hostile stance toward spiritual values was based on a careful assessment of fact. I overlooked the obvious fact—and was not told—that science does not have a God meter; that everything that counts cannot be counted; that some areas of existence lie, in principle, beyond science and are off limits to the dissections of the intellect.

Just as indigestion may follow a fine meal, the emphatic, presumptuous pronouncements of science against religion began to sour as time passed. I was particularly troubled by the rosy predictions of some of the leading scientists of the day. A great many of them believed science would somehow "save" humanity by rescuing it from illusion, fantasy, and false beliefs of all sorts. Although they seemed to know what science would save us *from* they were never clear about what science would save us *for*. Where was the evidence that the world would be a safer, saner, more fulfilling place to live if everyone would come around to thinking like materialistic scientists? True, throughout history untold nastiness has been committed in the name of religion, but what does science have to put in its place? If science succeeds in eradicating the religious impulse in human nature, most of our great art, architecture, and music would vanish, because it emerged from the depths of religious feeling. Science, even, arose from a spiritual motivation, the desire to have an unmediated confrontation with the real, as Needleman said.

Particularly vexing to me was the insistence by leading scientists that science should be morally neutral. There were titanic debates about whether or not scientists bore any responsibility for the detonation of the nuclear bombs at the conclusion of World War II. Some claimed their only responsibility was to investigate nature; how politicians used their findings was no concern of theirs. This argument struck me then, as now, as not only ethically and morally bankrupt, but—I choose the word carefully—insane. I recall feeling shamed on being exposed to this point of view. To me, science divorced from human concerns was an oxymoron. I gradually began to realize that something vital was missing. Science alone was no panacea for humanity. Unless supplemented by some other, higher vision, its claim for our allegiance was hollow.

Now, thirty years since my first exposure to these issues, there seems to be a greater opportunity than ever for science and spirituality to interpenetrate and make peace. Some scientists see openings for free will, values, and purposes, even the Almighty. The field of quantum physics, specifically the uncertainty principle, is particularly attractive to many of these scientists. Since the microworld is indeterminate, so the reasoning goes, this is an entry point for human choice-making and free will. Others see promising implications in chaos theory and nonlinear dynamics—the possibility that order can emerge out of chaos; that initial conditions, no matter how precisely defined, cannot predict future states; that "strange attractors" imply an inherent goal-directedness in nature.

As exciting as these developments are, I have never been able to find much philosophical and spiritual comfort in them. The main reason is that they *are* developments. "New" physics is more properly the "newest" physics, which will be superseded by a "newer" physics. A new science *will* arise. To base one's spiritual views on the shifting sands of science seems precarious in the extreme, no matter how tempting it is to do so.

Except in one sense. There are limits of knowledge within science. These limitations, as the logician Kurt Gödel showed, are profound and appear to be utterly fundamental.[2] The implications for science and religion are stunning. As philosopher Ken Wilber puts it in his book, *Quantum Questions: Mystical Writings of the World's Great Physicists*:

> . . . whereas classical physics was theoretically *hostile* to religion, modern physics is simply *indifferent* to it—it leaves so many theoretical holes in the universe that you may (or may not) fill them with religious substance, but if you do, it must be on philosophic or religious grounds. Physics cannot help you in the least, but it no longer objects to your efforts. . . . Physics does not support mysticism, but it no longer denies it. . . . This view . . . is probably the strongest and most revolutionary conclusion *vis à vis* religion that has ever been "officially" advanced by theoretical science itself. It is a monumental and epochal turning point in science's stance towards religion; it seems highly unlikely it will ever be reversed, since it is logical and not empirical in nature (or *a priori* and not *a posteriori*); therefore, it, in all likelihood, marks final closure on that most nagging aspect of the age-old debate between the physical sciences and religion (or the geist-sciences). What more could one possibly want?[3]

I subscribe to this view enthusiastically. The probes of science extend just so far, yet our intuition tells us there is more. What lies beyond? Science cannot tell us. The Absolute is *trans*-science, as the eminent Indian physicist D. S. Kothari put it.[4] Science opens a door through which we may (or may not) glimpse the Absolute. It gives us a glimpse, never a final picture. It is as if our scientific instruments are too fragile to endure the searing light of the Real. A Sufi saying has it, "No man has seen God and lived" including, we may presume, scientists.

The practice of medicine has provided me a unique perspective on the limitations of science. In fact, clinical medicine is a good antidote to the hubris and arrogance that often infect science. As the late physician, Lewis Thomas, director of research at Sloan-Kettering, once said, the most important discovery of the twentieth century is human igno-rance.[5] As a physician, I have seen many therapies come and go, each heralded as an ultimate intervention when first introduced. In addi-tion, the history of medicine is replete with a variety of theories of dis-ease causation, each of which was fervently believed in its day to be the final word.

But one can overemphasize the limitations of science. I am con-vinced that empirical science has much to contribute to the welfare of the human race, and that the scientific method remains a valuable way of guarding against some forms of self-delusion.

Although science provides us with valuable ways of *knowing,* it has not been much help in teaching us ways of *being.* It has proved virtu-ally useless as a method of improving character, including the character of those who practice it. I know of no evidence that scientists are morally or ethically superior to people who know nothing of science. As a guide to human conduct, science generally provides us with a poor harvest.

I have been troubled that we physicians, like scientists in general, have not always behaved admirably. As a single example, when Ignaz Philipp Semmelweis proposed in Vienna in the mid-1800s that physi-cians should wash their hands before delivering babies, he was excori-ated by his colleagues. Their skepticism was understandable; no one had ever seen a bacterium at the time. They demanded proof, which was not long in coming. With handwashing, Semmelweis reduced the death rate in women following childbirth by 1,000 percent. In spite of this data, he continued to be ridiculed. He fled Vienna for Budapest, where he eventually became insane as a result of the continuing harass-ment. This shameful episode shows that scientists are humans first and scientists later. Although we scientists like to claim the moral high ground, it is difficult historically to do so. Unless science can do so, it is difficult to see how its claim as a benchmark in the ordering of human societies can ever be taken seriously.

Events such as this, all too common in the history of science, re-flect one of my personal disappointments through the years—the ten-dency of some scientists to dismiss innovations in certain areas without a fair hearing or with no hearing. Scientists, like everyone else, can become so enamored of the status quo that we resist change and blindly defend theories currently in place. Historians have described the problem of "premature discovery" in science—developments that are so dissonant with current thinking that they do not fit in and are shoved aside.

Conservatism in science serves a valuable purpose; it prevents radical swings of the pendulum. But conservatism can be pathological and can stifle progress. Perhaps the most dramatic current example is in the domain of consciousness research. Over the past two decades, discoveries have shed new light on the nature of consciousness and its relationship to the material brain and body. These developments have affirmed for me a vision of the world that is inherently spiritual, and have contributed immeasurably to my mental peace. Consciousness research is a potential stage on which science and religion can finally, at long last, come together in harmony. If these developments are allowed to progress, we shall see a view of life, consciousness, and nature that is as glorious as any that has arisen in any of the major religions.

Currently, almost all scientists subscribe to a view of consciousness in which the mind is equated with the electrochemical processes of the brain. This materialistic view of consciousness is dismal, and is one of the major barriers preventing a meaningful dialogue between science and religion. It leads to the conclusion that death is final, that notions of the soul are illusory, and that the experience of "the spiritual" is nothing more than a result of the behavior of atoms in the brain.

An impressive body of evidence suggests that this view is simply wrong. The actions of consciousness cannot be accounted for by ascribing them only to brain processes. In brief, the evidence from consciousness research indicates that consciousness can do things that brains can't do. The brain is a "local" phenomenon, a physical entity confined to specific points in space and time. It cannot account for the findings of scores of investigators in laboratories all over the world that consciousness can manifest *nonlocally*, at remote distances from the brain, without the mediation of any known form of conventional energy. Carefully controlled studies demonstrate various forms of anomalous cognition, referred to in times past as telepathy, clairvoyance, and precognition.

It has been my good fortune to have experienced many of these events personally; therefore, my attitude toward these phenomena rests on the twin foundations of experience and scientifically demonstrable fact. These events show that consciousness cannot be confined to specific points in space, such as the brain or body, or time, such as the present moment.

The implications of a nonlocal aspect of the mind are stunning. "Nonlocal" does not suggest "quite large" or "a very long time." Nonlocality implies infinitude in space and time, because a *limited nonlocality is a contradiction in terms*. Therefore, if some aspect of the mind is genuinely nonlocal, as the empirical evidence suggests, we come to a surprising conclusion: some aspect of our consciousness is infinite in space and time, therefore eternal and immortal.

These findings also have surprising implications for our relationship with the Absolute—God, Goddess, Allah, the Universe, however the Ultimate is defined. Infinitude in space (omnipresence) and time (eternality) are qualities we have always attributed to the Absolute. These qualities belong, then, *both* to humans and the Absolute. We appear to share qualities with the Divine, called by many spiritual traditions "the God within."

Empirical science therefore provides us with indirect evidence for the soul—a nonlocal aspect of consciousness that is infinite in space and time, that is immortal, that is unconfined to the brain, and that is *more* than the physical brain and body.

We should not underestimate the significance of these findings. We have always said that belief in the soul is irrational; there is no proof. Today we stand at a landmark point in human history when, for the very first time, we have indirect evidence for the soul—a nonlocal aspect of consciousness—erupting in laboratories around the world.[6]

We should not overlook the irony in these observations. Science, the perennial enemy of religion and spirituality, seems to be shooting itself in the foot by producing evidence that many of the concepts it has opposed, such as the soul, may in fact be true.

Not only does the nonlocal view of consciousness connect us with the Absolute, it unites us with each other. It has come as a great consolation to me to discover that this idea has been arrived at by some of the greatest scientists in this century. The Nobel physicist Erwin Schrödinger, for example, spoke of the "one mind"—the unity of consciousness implied by a mind that is nonlocal, that knows no boundaries. According to Schrödinger:

> There is obviously only one alternative, namely the unification of minds or consciousness. Their multiplicity is only apparent, in truth there is only one mind. . . . In all the world, there is no kind of framework within which we can find consciousness in the plural. . . . Mind by its very nature is a *singulare tantum*. I should say: the overall number of minds is just one.[7]

One nonlocal manifestation of the mind is of particular interest to me—distant, intercessory prayer. The evidence for the distant, positive effects of empathic intentionality, often called prayer by those who engage in it, is abundant. Some of the experiments in this area are fanatically precise. They deal with the effects of distant prayer not just in humans but also in lower organisms, seeds, and plants as well, which makes it impossible in principle to ascribe these effects to positive thinking, suggestion, expectation, or placebo responses.

I believe that the evidence for intercessory prayer may catalyze a truce between science and religion. The evidence also may make possible greater tolerance between the world's religions, which we desperately need. This is because the experiments in prayer reveal that the prayers of all religions work. No religion, therefore, can claim a monopoly on prayer. Science thus universalizes and democratizes prayer, and is therefore an enemy to narrowness and intolerance. This is one of the greatest contributions science can possibly make, in my judgment, to human welfare.[8]

I am encouraged by the current attempts within science to account for nonlocal manifestations of consciousness. Nobel physicist Brian Josephson proposes that developments within modern physics in the area of nonlocality will account eventually for the nonlocal manifestations of consciousness.[9] Subatomic particles behave nonlocally; minds also behave nonlocally; but whether nonlocality at the subatomic level has anything whatever to do with nonlocality at the level of consciousness is completely unknown. However, the fact that physicists have recognized nonlocal events in laboratory experiments should grant a permission of sorts for us to explore whether these events *might* be connected in some way with the nonlocal expressions of the mind.

I believe that radically new ways of imagining consciousness will be necessary, perhaps along the lines proposed by mathematician and philosopher David J. Chalmers. He suggests that consciousness is a fundamental, irreducible feature of nature, perhaps on a par with matter and energy.[10] Will we ever know how consciousness manifests nonlocally? The absence of an explanatory model should not prevent us from honoring the data flowing from consciousness research. In science and medicine we often know that something happens before we understand how.

Philosopher Eugene Mills states that when Sir Isaac Newton invoked gravity, that "mysterious force," he was attacked by his contemporaries for surrendering to mysticism. They disapproved of his failure to explain why physical bodies behaved in accordance with his laws, or how distant bodies could act on one another. This sort of worry no longer bothers us, Mills states, but not because we have answered the questions.[11] Our fundamental attitude has changed. So it may be with the idea of nonlocal mind. One day the nonlocal nature of consciousness may seem so natural that we simply cease to struggle with it. This brings to mind an old saying: Physicists never really understand a new theory, they just get used to it.

Looking back, I believe that materialism is one of the most powerful forces ever to grip the mind of human beings. It can be spellbinding, literally, and force aside any other competing point of view. It is said that Kepler, the astronomer, having been unhappy in his first marriage, resolved to choose his second wife on scientific principles. He made a list of all his female acquaintances and eliminated all but eleven of them. Then he analyzed these eleven, setting down in parallel columns their merits and defects. When he concluded his tabulations, he married the lady whose data displayed the greatest predominance of merit over defect. Alas, this marriage suffered the same fate as the first; at which point Kepler pronounced the problem insoluble to human reason.

This story may be apocryphal, but the materialistic view can undoubtedly suffocate the human spirit. Darwin, in his autobiography, lamented that his mind "seems to have become a kind of machine for grinding general laws out of large collections of facts." His solution: ". . . if I had to live my life again I would have made a rule to read some poetry and listen to some music at least once every week. . . . The loss of these tastes is a loss of happiness, and may possibly be injurious to the intellect, and more probably to the moral character, by enfeebling the emotional part of our nature."[12] I agree with Darwin that science can squeeze the juice out of life. That is why I carry a small volume of Whitman's poetry wherever I go. It has been my traveling companion for years. When on the road, I begin my day by opening the book at random and reading whatever passage catches my eye. The "selection" is usually uncannily appropriate to the task at hand. In addition, I have learned to make a place for constant connection with nature. My wife and I live on the side of a mountain with coyotes and deer in an excruciatingly beautiful setting in northern New Mexico. I feel these influences have helped protect against the constrictions of the intellect which Darwin described.

My wife has been a sustaining and grounding presence all my life. My spiritual journey has been smoothed by her support. The steps I have taken have always been with her; we have left our tracks together.

The Dalai Lama has said: "My religion is simple. My religion is kindness." This expresses my current attitude toward religion, a minimalist approach as far as outward forms go. I prefer my religion unadorned, a mystery unsolved, a place on the map not filled in. So I do not belong to any particular religious organization. I do not advocate this approach; it simply reflects my own unique journey, which will be unlike that of anyone else. For me, the task is to listen to the messages my blood whispers to me, as Hermann Hesse put it, during meditation, prayer, and contemplation. Although most people would probably find this spartan approach unsatisfying, it is deeply nourishing to me.

Honoring the great unknowns and living with uncertainty are important to me. Along these lines, Joseph Campbell once said that we must get rid of the life we've planned, so as to have the life that is waiting for us. This may apply as well to our religious life. If we fill it up, what else can enter? Meister Eckhart's words ring true for me: "Whoever perceives something in God and attaches thereby some name to him, that is not God. God is . . . ineffable. . . . It is God's nature to be without a nature."

The void Eckhart saw is a holy space. It is, of course, far from empty. Like the vacuum studied by physicists, it is where the action is.

The Grail Legend, says Campbell, is the most influential legend of the western mind. In Campbell's version, King Arthur's knights were gathered at table for a banquet, but the king would not allow the banquet to proceed until an auspicious event had occurred. Suddenly the Grail appeared, hovering over the table, but it was draped and could not be fully seen. Then it disappeared. Gawain, Arthur's nephew, proposed that the knights go on a quest to find the Grail and see it fully. The knights agreed, but realized that it would be improper to venture forth in a group. They therefore resolved to go forth singly and to enter the forest where it was darkest, where there was no light, no path, and no guide.

If a reader is tempted to follow precisely the path of any of the contributors to this book, as if it constitutes some formula, this inclination ought to be set aside. Not only are our paths unique, our journeys must be begun alone, our great myths tell us. That does not mean we shouldn't listen to wise counsel before embarking, or that the journey will remain solitary. Once the forest is entered, wise guides may appear; fellow travelers are often encountered; miracles occur. But the decision to go on a journey is an act of courage, and no one can make it for us.

May we meet along the way.

References

1. Jacob Needleman, *A Sense of the Cosmos: The Encounter of Modern Science and Ancient Truth* (Garden City, N.Y.: Doubleday & Company, Inc., 1975), 166–170.

2. Larry Dossey, "Gödel's Theorem," in *Space, Time & Medicine* (Boston: Shambhala, 1982), 192–198.

3. Ken Wilber, *Quantum Questions: Mystical Writings of the World's Great Physicists* (Boston: Shambhala, 1984), 169–170.

4. D. S. Kothari, "Atom and Self" (The Mehnad Saha Medal Lecture–1978 published in *Proceedings of the Indian National Academy of Science*, Part A, Physical Science, 1980; 46[1]), 1–28.

5. Lewis Thomas, *The Medusa and the Snail* (New York: Bantam, 1983). Quoted in *Noetic Sciences Review* (Autumn 1994, no. 31), 48.

6. For an introduction to the concept of nonlocality in modern physics, and the potential relevance of this idea to consciousness, the following books are recommended for the lay reader:
   Nick Herbert, *Quantum Reality* (New York: Dutton, 1986);
   Nick Herbert, *Elemental Mind* (New York: Dutton, 1993).

7. Erwin Schrödinger, *What Is Life? and Mind and Matter* (London: Cambridge University Press, 1969): 31–34, 139.

8. For a look at the role of prayer in medicine, and a review of the evidence in this area, the following sources are recommended:
   Daniel Benor, *Healing Research* I (Munich: Helix Verlag, 1993);
   Larry Dossey, *Healing Words: The Power of Prayer and the Practice of Medicine* (San Francisco: HarperSanFrancisco, 1993);
   Larry Dossey, *Prayer Is Good Medicine* (San Francisco: HarperSanFrancisco, 1996);
   Larry Dossey, *Be Careful What You Pray For . . . You Just Might Get It* (San Francisco: HarperSanFrancisco, 1997);
   Larry Dossey, "The Return of Prayer," *Alternative Therapies in Health and Medicine* 3, no. 6 (1997): 10ff;
   David B. Larson and Mary A. Greenwold Milano, "Are Religion and Spirituality Clinically Relevant in Health Care?" *Mind/Body Medicine* 1, no. 3 (1995): 147–57;
   Jeffrey S. Levin, David B. Larson, and Christina M. Puchalski, "Religion and Spirituality in Medicine: Research and Education," *Journal of the American Medical Association* 278, no. 9 (1997), 792;
   Jeffrey S. Levin, "How Prayer Heals: A Theoretical Model," *Alternative Therapies in Health and Medicine* 2, no. 1 (1996), 66–73;
   Elisabeth Targ, "Evaluating Distant Healing: A Research Review," *Alternative Therapies in Health and Medicine* 2, no. 1 (1996), 74–78.

9. Brian Josephson and F. Pallikara-Viras, "Biological Utilization of Quantum Nonlocality," *Foundations of Physics* 21 (1991), 197–207.

10. David J. Chalmers, "The Puzzle of Conscious Experience," *Scientific American* 273, no. 6 (1995), 80–86.

11. Eugene Mills, "Giving Up on the Hard Problem," *Journal of Consciousness Studies* 3, no. 1 (1996), 26–32.

12. *The Autobiography of Charles Darwin,* cited in *Healing Arts* 2, no. 1 (1996), 31.

4

ON UNDERSTANDING SCIENCE

FROM A PERSPECTIVE OF FAITH

OWEN GINGERICH

"**I**t's curious," a senior historian of science remarked to me recently, "how many of our students come to us from rather conservative religious backgrounds."

Coming to terms with science and the claims made on its behalf has clearly posed a challenge to several generations of budding young intellectuals whose roots were nourished by religious communities that had themselves sorted out neither the higher criticism of the last century-and-a-half nor the periodic scientific upheavals since Copernicus. For many of us, the long historical process of the Scientific Revolution and the Enlightenment has replayed itself in real twentieth-century time in our own church environments.

The Copernican revolution is now four centuries old, and it would be astonishing indeed to find a church or synagogue that teaches a cosmology with an immobile, central earth surrounded by crystalline planetary spheres. But there must be many Sunday School teachers who (as I can verify from personal experience) still agree with Isaac Newton that Adam lived about six thousand years ago, and there are many who would accept the notions of Newton's protégé and successor, William Whiston, who argued that the principal geological features of the earth were carved by the Noachan deluge.

As a young undergraduate chemistry major at a small, midwestern

Mennonite college, I daily passed by the two busts decorating the foyer of our Science Hall, those of Isaac Newton and Louis Agassiz. I could understand the choice of Isaac Newton, the preeminent physicist and one of the three greatest mathematicians of all time. But why the Swiss paleontologist Louis Agassiz? Not until years later, when I had intensified my reading in history of science, did I come to understand that Agassiz was an articulate opponent of Darwin's theory of evolution, a theory that was given the total silent treatment by our college.

Today the history of science landscape is dotted with scholars who are attempting to come to terms with their early religious environments. Ronald Number's perceptive account, *The Creationists,* stems in part from the tensions arising from his Seventh-Day Adventist upbringing. James Moore's researches, which have demonstrated that the resistance to Darwin's ideas cuts right across religious and materialistic lines, were motivated by his evangelical roots. My own studies of Kepler and the Copernican revolutions were inspired by a curiosity about the idea of creation and the nature of science that grew out of counterclaims from some of the books on the shelves of the Goshen College library.

Yet I have always been extremely grateful for my long Anabaptist heritage, my liberal arts education in a church school, and a nourishing Christian home environment. It has been from this springboard that I have made my way in astronomy and in the history of science, with the ever more passionate desire to understand how science achieves its claims to reverence and credibility.

My initial fascination with astronomy came earlier than I myself remember. On a stiflingly hot night, with the temperature inside our house still over one hundred degrees, my mother moved cots into the backyard.

"What are those?" I, as a five-year-old, am said to have asked.

"Those are stars, dear. You've often seen them."

"But I didn't know they stayed out all night!"

My interest in the stars already kindled, my father did his best to encourage it. He was a remarkable man, really, whose great-grandfathers had all been Amish bishops. The eldest child on an Iowa farm, he was the only one of his five siblings to go to high school, but he went on to earn a doctorate in American cultural history, writing a thesis on the Mennonites in Iowa. It was while he was working on his Ph.D. on weekends at the University of Iowa that he would occasionally bring back an astronomy book for me. In the depression era these were precious luxuries, something he could little afford, but perhaps tokens of penance for his frequent absence at the university.

My father took time to help build me a telescope made from a long mailing tube, a ten-cent-store magnifier, and a lens extracted from a cigar box full of discarded eyeglass lenses borrowed from a local optometrist. I still remember how awed I was that he knew how to test their focal lengths to select just the right lens. How proud I was to show our fifth-grade teacher the rings of Saturn! A few years later, I was again impressed when my father adapted the telescope into a telephoto camera to photograph a partial eclipse of the sun.

As my father's academic interests carried him further from his rural roots, his allegiance to his Mennonite heritage remained vital. In an article on the menace of propaganda and how to meet it published in the *Mennonite Quarterly Review,* he warned against the rabble-rousing of Gerald Winrod, whose hate-mongering ministry was capturing some interest among the simple Mennonite folk. He told me that Winrod threatened a lawsuit if the journal refused to print a retraction, but in the event, the editors held their ground. (Within two decades my father would become the managing editor of the *MQR.*) Meanwhile, my father's public lectures on behalf of Christian pacifism as well as his critique of antisemitic propaganda brought him little sympathy from the super-patriot WASPs on the school board of the small Republican town where he was teaching. His contract was not renewed, but when my mother collapsed in a nervous breakdown, the board generously beat a retreat, saying that with his Ph.D. my father was overqualified, and that they had merely been trying to propel him into a more appropriate position. A year later he unexpectedly received a call from a Mennonite college in Kansas to take a position as assistant professor of history.

We had been in Kansas only three months when the Japanese launched their attack on Pearl Harbor. "This will not be over soon," I announced to my sixth-grade classmates, undoubtedly mirroring opinions I had picked up at home. Patriotic fervor swept the community and the school system. There were scrap drives and war bond drives and much assembly singing of military songs. Even the Mennonites, with their long pacifist heritage, were divided. Some young men, influenced by their high school friends, opted for noncombatant military service, while others were eventually sent off to nonpaying work camps as religious conscientious objectors. In an effort to provide an environment conducive to traditional Mennonite values, a secondary school academy was hastily organized on the college campus where we were living. In the most agonizing decision of my life I elected not to enroll in the academy but to continue at the high school, where I could study Latin, chemistry, and physics. Taking the role of an outsider had its unpleasant moments, and I decided to cut it short by signing up for a summer correspondence course so that I would have enough credits to enroll in college a year early. The discipline of working on that course in all sorts of unlikely venues has stayed with me, and even now I find distant hotel rooms and unfamiliar libraries congenial places for writing essays like this one.

Meanwhile, the war finally ended, and a marvelous opportunity opened up for young Mennonite farm boys. The fledgling United Nations Relief and Rehabilitation Agency inaugurated a program to send horses to war-torn Europe, and they needed seagoing cowboys to accompany the shipments. I was not a farm boy, nor were many of the young men that my father recruited for a crew of thirty-two potential cowhands. Nevertheless, in 1946, some thirty of us served as seagoing cowboys aboard the *Stephen R. Mallory*, a converted liberty ship that carried nearly eight hundred horses from Newport News to a devastated Poland. Fifty years later we gathered for a reunion. By definition, we were all by now senior citizens, but at the time of the trip at least half of us had been sixteen- or seventeen-year-olds. Looking back to those immediate post-war years, we wondered what had induced our parents to let a gang of mostly teenagers go off on such an extraordinary adventure. The answer seemed clearly that it was confidence in my father, who had seized a remarkable travel opportunity, who had organized the crew, and who went along as UNRRA supervisor.

For me, the voyage was an eye-opening exposure to the seamy underside of the real world: sailors whose every sentence was salted with the f-word, a shattered and ruined Gdansk, rampant prostitution, and black-marketeering in the Polish port. But the trip also had unimagined consequences in molding my professional career. Two decades after that memorable journey, I mentioned it to a Polish colleague at an international astronomical meeting; he in turn urged me to return to Poland by attending the forthcoming history of science congress there.

One thing led to another. I was appointed to the committee to plan the international commemoration of the five hundredth anniversary of the birth of Nicolaus Copernicus, the Polish astronomer who in 1543 stopped the sun and threw the earth into dizzying motion. In due time I was invited to give the keynote discourse for the International Astronomical Union's Extraordinary General Assembly in Warsaw to celebrate Copernicus and his heliocentric blueprint for the cosmos. But this was only the beginning, for, as my interests turned more decisively from astrophysics to history of science, I became involved in a census of surviving copies of Copernicus's pioneering treatise, *De revolutionibus*. While the printed books are as alike as peas in a pod, the marginal annotations made by sixteenth-century owners reveal much about early reactions to the book.

Between the voyage to Gdansk and my return there twenty years later, I had struggled with the decision to become an astronomer. Martin Luther, like the apostle Paul centuries earlier, had taught that one could be a Christian in whatever work one found oneself. In those bygone days "like father, like son" tended to be the rule, and selecting life's work was less of a choice than an inflexible expectation. But, at Goshen College, with its motto of "Culture for Service," we were continually reminded that most of us faced real choices as to how to invest our lives. Astronomy did not seem high on the list. It was hard to think of a respectable profession more useless for the unwashed crush of humanity. Perhaps a career as a chemist could produce medicines or plastics of benefit to the human race.

"If you really want to become an astronomer," advised my mathematics professor, "you ought to go for it. We shouldn't let the atheists take over any field." Heartened by his encouraging words, I enrolled in the Harvard graduate school, hoping to find out more about my favorite science and envisioning employment perhaps as a science journalist.

Not since the 1920s had Harvard admitted a graduate student from Goshen College, so, to be safe, the Department of Astronomy accepted me only for a master's degree. In due course I qualified for the M.A., and was automatically transferred to the Ph.D. program, but my draft board had other ideas. They had given me a student deferment for an M.A. and that was that. They were now determined that I should pay my dues to the Selective Service System. In that era student deferments were endemic, but I was a religious conscientious objector, an unpopular position with the Goshen, Indiana, draft board. After two years of bureaucratic bungling, a full F.B.I. investigation, and treading water in graduate school, I was finally drafted and sent to teach at the American University of Beirut. I wasn't entirely pleased with this turn of events. Beirut promised to be a fascinating locale for me (and my bride of a year, a former classmate from Goshen) but the interruption of my graduate program seemed devastating.

In retrospect, I see God moving in mysterious ways. Three years later, when I returned to Harvard, the landscape had been transfigured. The Russians had launched Sputnik, the United States had been thrust into the space age, the Smithsonian Astrophysical Observatory had joined forces with Harvard Observatory, and their satellite tracking program had procured the most powerful electronic computer in New England. I took to computer programming like a duck to water, and was soon immersed in a trail-blazing thesis, crunching numbers that could scarcely be subdued with hand calculation, ascertaining the way in which the many-colored radiation of light flowed through the foggy outer layers of stars. Without that seemingly unwelcome detour to Beirut, this would never have happened.

The Smithsonian Observatory not only had the equipment to get me into the vanguard of high-speed astronomical computing, but it also had a major communications center to connect the satellite tracking stations throughout the world. This led to my becoming the head of the Central Bureau for Astronomical Telegrams, the arm of the

International Astronomical Union that names comets and generally disseminates information about transient astronomical phenomena, and which was looking for a new home after being located for many decades in Copenhagen. I moved the Bureau to Cambridge. During my tenure as director, pulsars were discovered; the prompt announcements of their positions gave a considerable impetus to the study of these high-density stars. Simply because I signed the telegrams and announcement cards, I became well known in the astronomical world.

The detour to Beirut had another unexpected but happy consequence as well. A year after I had completed my thesis, the teaching slot for the astronomy department's offering in the Harvard General Education program became vacant rather late in the cycle of academic appointments and, as an experienced and obviously available teacher, I was asked to take it over. More than thirty years later I am still teaching "The Astronomical Perspective," and I believe it is the longest-running course at Harvard still under the same management.

With respect to religious belief at a secular university, there is a curious but well-established asymmetry. Atheist professors can and frequently do voice their personal views in their courses, but to mention one's Christian beliefs in a comparably forcible way would no doubt bring charges of proselytizing. However, the traditional but rather sparsely attended "morning prayers" at Harvard do allow a pulpit for one's religious convictions, and I have spoken there almost annually since the 1960s.

Very early in my teaching career at Harvard a more senior professor warned me against allowing students to write essays on religious issues. "If the paper is rotten and you give it the grade it deserves, the student will feel personally attacked for his religious beliefs." It took some years for me to get the courage to include such topics on the standard essay list, but I knew that some of these issues were intensely discussed in dormitory bull sessions, and I felt a responsibility to inform students of a very serious and substantial literature that deserves consideration. When I announced that I would myself grade the papers on "Is there a conflict between science and the idea of a personal God?" nearly half the class elected that topic. A teaching assistant independently evaluated the papers, the consistency of grading was remarkable, and no one complained about the assigned grades. Perhaps my report of this experience to the faculty during the debate on the establishment of an undergraduate major in religion helped persuade my fellow Harvard professors to vote yes.

During the 1960s my long-latent interest in the history of astronomy began to emerge. As I used ever more powerful computers for my astrophysics researches, it occurred to me that the IBM 7094 could make a nice demonstration of one of Kepler's particularly tedious problems. Kepler complained that his initial attempt to determine an orbit for the planet Mars had cost him at least seventy tries. The computer handily solved it in the minimum possible number, nine iterations. Electronic computers were then still something of a novelty, and my account, "The Computer Versus Kepler," received unexpectedly wide publicity.

Kepler's life and work had fascinated me ever since I had read Arthur Koestler's *The Sleepwalkers* shortly after its 1958 publication. A deeply religious thinker, Kepler found inspiration for his cosmic harmonies in his Protestant Christianity. In his works he would frequently burst into psalms or prayers such as the one that concludes his *Harmonice mundi:*

> I give Thee thanks, O Lord Creator, because I have delighted in thy handiwork and I have exulted in the works of thy hands. Behold! now, I have completed the work of my profession, having used as much of the ability as Thou hast given me; to those who will read these demonstrations, I have made manifest the glory of thy works, insofar as the narrows of my mind could grasp its infinity. My intellect has been prepared for the most faultless philosophizing: if anything unworthy of thy designs, which Thou dost wish men to know, has been put forth by me, inspire me also so that I may set it right. If I have been allured into brashness by the wonderful beauty of thy works or if I have loved my own glory among men, while advancing in work destined for thy glory, gently and mercifully pardon me: and finally, deign graciously to cause that these demonstrations may lead to thy glory and to the salvation of souls, and nowhere be an obstacle to that. Amen.

In that sectarian age, Kepler's staunch belief that Calvinists should be treated as Christian brothers did not sit well with the Lutheran professors at his alma mater, effectively preventing him from getting a position there at Tübingen. And his refusal to find fault with the "popish" Gregorian calendar did not win him any points with his astronomy mentor, Michael Maestlin. At one point, when Kepler was working in Catholic territory, he sent his son away with friends so that he could honestly say he did not know where young Ludwig was when the authorities tried to force his son to take the Catholic catechism. Kepler suffered much for his independent but deeply sincere religious thinking; eventually he was excommunicated by the local pastor because of his reservations about certain doctrines in the Lutheran Formula of Concord.

Both as an astronomer and as a Christian I could not help but admire Kepler's beliefs as well as his trail-blazing astronomical achievements. In 1971 we observed the four hundredth anniversary of Kepler's birth, and for that occasion I prepared seven papers on different aspects of his work, including an important follow-up on my earlier computer-versus-Kepler paper. With the 1973 Copernican quinquecentennial on the horizon, the die was cast, and I turned increasingly to the history of astronomy. As I cheerfully assured my astrophysicist friends, I was the victim of anniversaries.

Nevertheless, my intense involvement with astrophysical calculations of model stellar atmospheres, and the challenging problem of actually matching the calculations against real stellar spectra, had given me considerable insight into the way scientific judgments are made. The power of science, I gradually realized, lay not so much in great proofs as in the little threads woven together to form the grand tapestry of understanding. It was the beauty of all the small parts fitting together in a way that made sense, an intricate texture making a grand design.

As I read more and more intensively in science's history, this view of science, that is, the role of coherence and understanding, became ever clearer. And thus it was, in 1982 when I was asked to inaugurate the new Dwight Lecture in Christian Thought at the University of Pennsylvania, I was intellectually prepared to describe the making of the great tapestry of science within a Christian framework—it was to become my "pro-Christianity, anti-Creationism lecture."

One unanticipated hazard still lay between my acceptance and the lectureship: the sponsors asked me to sign a statement of faith containing, among other things, a phrase specifying the "unique, divine inspiration, entire trust-worthiness and authority of the Bible." Probably when I was an undergraduate at Goshen College I would have signed the statement without blanching, but in the meantime the expression had become a code word for a literalist interpretation of the Scriptures that I had difficulty accepting. I had long since adopted the stance advocated implicitly by Kepler and explicitly by Galileo that "the Bible tells how to go to heaven, not how the heavens go." In other words, the Bible is not a scientific textbook, but an account of salvation history.

As I was to explain in my Dwight Lecture, science is, by its very nature, godless. It is a mechanistic system, contrived to show how things work, and unable to say anything about the who, the designer. I remarked that I understood how some people feel threatened by the ascendancy of a system of looking at the world that does not explicitly include the designing hand of God in the construction, and that I could sympathize if a deeply religious person finds this incomplete and unsatisfying. I added that I could even sympathize mildly with the frustration of the creationists, who wish that some broader philosophical framework could be placed into biology textbooks. But, I said, they are mistaken when they take scientific explanations, as such, to be antigod or atheistic, they are wrong when they think that the Genesis account can substitute for the "how" of scientific explanations, and they err when they think that a meaningful tack is to brand evolution as a "mere hypothesis." In a certain sense all the theoretical explanations of science, the weft that holds the tapestry together, are hypotheses, and to unthread one section risks destroying the entire fabric.

Since I was uncomfortable in signing the specific statement of faith proposed by the sponsors of the Dwight Lecture, I decided to offer them an alternative. Here is where belonging to a community of faith was very helpful. I sketched out a credo, and then brought it to several of my fellow members of the Mennonite Congregation of Boston. After some discussion, here is the form it took:

GOD AS CREATOR
I believe in God as the superintelligence who planned and guided the creation of the universe, as revealed in the remarkable details of the natural world and as attested in the Bible.

TO BE HUMAN IS TO ACCEPT RESPONSIBILITY

I believe that the creation of humanity is a principal purpose of the universe and that humankind was created in the image of God, particularly with respect to consciousness, conscience, and the moral freedom to choose right or wrong.

GOD PERSONIFIED THROUGH CHRIST

I believe that God continues to act within history as seen in the record of the Old Testament, and as demonstrated in the life and death of Jesus Christ, which is attested by the record of the New Testament. I believe, with my Anabaptist forebears, that we are called by Jesus to a life of discipleship that, through sacrificial love and forgiving reconciliation, witnesses to God's love for us and to the community of men and women.

GOD AS CONTINUING INSPIRATION

I believe in the efficacy of the Holy Spirit in sensitizing our consciences, and through the discerning interaction of believers, in guiding us to an ever renewed understanding of the revelation of God through the Holy Scriptures.

In its various forms, the Dwight Lecture, "Let There Be Light: Modern Cosmogony and Biblical Creation," was ultimately to gain a greater dissemination than I or the sponsors of the lecture had ever dreamed possible. I have given the lecture more than forty times, mostly in college and university settings, one of which was recorded by the "Ideas" program of the Canadian Broadcasting System, which aired it several times coast-to-coast in Canada. Roland Frye (distinguished literary historian and theologian at the University of Pennsylvania) included it in his collection, *Is God a Creationist?* and Timothy Ferris anthologized it in *The World Treasury of Physics, Astronomy, and Mathematics,* which became a principal selection of the Book-of-the-Month Club.

Subsequently Roland Frye invited me to join the advisory board of the Center of Theological Inquiry in Princeton, a theological think tank whose brief included the relation of science to Christianity. The Center brings together some distinguished theologians and scientists, both in its advisory board and in a special annual consultation that has provided some of my most intense intellectual and spiritual stimulation of recent years. The Center sponsored a further lecture of mine,

"Kepler's Anguish and Hawking's Query: Reflections on Natural Theology," which was in a sense a sequel to the Dwight Lecture. The CTI lecture in turn was published in *Great Ideas Today,* the yearbook of the *Great Books of the Western World.* The two lectures have firmly identified me as a scientist willing to confront questions at the intersection of faith and science, so that when organizers of conferences on this topic say "round up the usual suspects," I often find myself invited.

A typical situation arose recently when a group of NASA researchers announced that they had found evidence for primitive fossil life in a meteorite from Mars. Reporters from the *Philadelphia Inquirer,* the *Christian Science Monitor, Newsweek,* and others wanted a theological spin for their stories. "The universe could be creeping with microbes," I declared, "and it wouldn't make any theological difference. Traditional Christianity has considered mankind the pinnacle of God's creation within the physical universe. It is true the human brain is the most complex object known to us—in comparison, a stellar interior or a supernova explosion is trivially simple. But the human brain gives us power of imagination, to think beyond ourselves and to consider that within this vast cosmos there could be beings more complex and more intelligent. I cannot think of any biblical requirement or theological constraint that would demand for us to be alone in the universe. Thus I believe we dare not limit God's creativity to the creation of humankind."

The whole question of the possibility of life on other worlds is closely bound up with views concerning the origin and evolution of life, and much of my quest to understand the nature of science has been bound up with the theory of biological evolution. Recently, Pope John Paul II has declared that evolution is not just a hypothesis. What he meant, of course, was that it was not, to use common parlance, a "mere hypothesis," that is, something that can be ignored or not taken seriously. In reality, much of the scientific view of nature is a grand hypothesis, a coherent web of explanation that is never "proved" in any formal sense. Biological evolution has many problems, but it is the only working framework that makes scientific sense of the historical and geographical distribution of species and of the staggering interrelatedness of the DNA genetic coding throughout the entire tree of life.

From time to time after one of my lectures I'm given a copy of the book *Life: How Did it Happen? Creation or Evolution?* I always tell the donor that the book asks the wrong question. It can be both creation and evolution. The real question is, Accident or Purpose?

While such views can and do find occasional outlet through the media, some of my friends began to explore the possibilities of wider dissemination through television. If I spoke to an audience of a hundred every night between now and my retirement, I could hope to reach not more than 200,000 people; a series on public television would probably be seen by at least five million viewers. However, there is much more at stake: on the airwaves science is generally portrayed from a strictly materialistic perspective, as if the universe itself were godless. Would it not be informative to present science sympathetically from the theistic perspective of the Judeo-Christian heritage? Such a program would steer between the sterile biblical literalism of the creationists on the one hand, and flagrant materialistic atheism on the other. It would demonstrate that faith and science are by no means incompatible.

Foremost among the enthusiasts for this opportunity has been Robert Herrmann, sometime executive director of the American Scientific Affiliation, an organization of professional scientists who take both science and the Bible seriously. With start-up funds from the ASA, we teamed up with Geoff Haines-Stiles, one of the leading independent science television producers, to prepare scenarios for six episodes of a series entitled "Space, Time, and God." Our advisors included such people as Nobel physicist Charles Townes, cosmologist Alan Sandage, science museum director David Ellis, theologian Langdon Gilkey, and Catholic educator Ted Hesburgh. As Haines-Stiles and I blocked out a truly educational set of programs with some unusual filming locales, we became convinced the we had scripted an interesting and telegenic series. The episodes illuminated the controversial "Galileo affair," explained the evidence for the vast distances and ages encountered in cosmology, explored the question of "are we alone?" and asked what it means to be human.

Unfortunately, quality "blockbuster" television is very expensive, and the production with its requisite publicity would cost more than

$300,000 per episode. Several wealthy but conservative Christians inquired about our designs, but when the word "evolution" was mentioned, they faded away. Corporations acted skittish for the same reasons that produce the curious asymmetry in academia: somehow it is acceptable to support a "personal view" of science that explicitly incorporates an anti-religious stance, but not a theistic perspective. Barring a small miracle, it seems that the series is not to be.

Despite such disappointments I have had many interesting although smaller forums for speaking of the relationship of science and faith. Some have been provided by the John Templeton Foundation, which has sponsored lectures in both congregational and academic settings. Others have come quite unexpectedly, such as an invitation to give an Advent sermon at the National Cathedral in Washington, D.C. Happily from my point of view, each time I have to restate where I stand in this spiritual pilgrimage, I clarify at least one more corner of the always incompletely defined body of what I truly believe.

5

WHAT I BELIEVE

PETER E. HODGSON

Mine is not a particularly dramatic story. I was baptized a few days after my birth and, by the grace of God, have remained in the church. My story is not one of dramatic conversion, but of gradually learning the faith and trying to live it.

My father was a member of the Church of England and my mother came from an old Catholic family that had held on to the faith through penal times. From my earliest years, I experienced the pain of religious separation. My father had clear ideas about right and wrong, and taught more by example than by articulated principles. He had a strong sense of duty to king and country, and insisted that one's word is one's bond. He faithfully kept his promise that I be brought up as a Catholic, and his integrity in this respect was much admired by my Catholic relations. He went to France in 1914 with his regiment, the Queen's Westminsters, and fought in the trenches throughout the Great War. Most of the regiment did not survive. In one of his rare observations on religion he remarked, "I'll say one thing for your Padres: they came over the top with us."

My mother's maiden name was Bulbeck, and her ancestors came to England with William the Conqueror. There is a town called Bolbec in Normandy, not far from the great abbey of Bec. The Bulbeck family was prosperous in the Middle Ages, and there is a village in Norfolk called Swaffam Bulbeck that is probably connected with it. When Henry the Eighth broke with Rome, the Catholic faith of England, so strong and vigorous, was brutally suppressed and heavy fines were imposed for nonattendance at the Protestant services. Catholics who refused to abandon their faith are called recusants, and there are Bulbecks on the Recusant Rolls for Hampshire. The Protestant reformers desecrated the English cathedrals and churches, smashed the statues, and burnt the vestments, as graphically described by Eamon Duffy in his recent book, *The Stripping of the Altars*.[1] It was high treason to say Mass, and priests like Edmund Campion, who ministered secretly to Catholics, were hung, drawn, and quartered at Tyburn, now Marble Arch, if they were caught. The Bulbeck family lost most of its possessions but retained its faith. Over the centuries the Church of England has mellowed, and is now a strong force for good in a secular world, but there is little memory of its origins and indeed it claims continuity with the medieval church. My father was astonished when I told him that our ancient cathedrals were built by Catholics and were Catholic for hundreds of years.

English Catholicism is characterized by unostentatious piety and devotion to the papacy. Partly this reticence is attributable to centuries of persecution, living for centuries as a *gens lucifuga,* partly to the English distrust of emotional excesses. It is difficult to illustrate this quiet matter-of-fact attitude to life. However, I recall one Sunday morning in the 1940s at about 7:45 in the morning when my mother and I were just about to leave home to attend Mass. Suddenly there was a tremendous explosion, followed soon after by the incoming scream of a supersonic V2 rocket that had landed a short distance in front of the house. The heavy front door flew open, the windows shattered, and a cloud of soot billowed out of the fireplace and into the living room. My father leaped out of bed and exclaimed, "What do we do now?" "We're just off to Mass," replied my mother calmly as if nothing whatever had happened, and off we went. She was not to be deflected one iota from her devotions by such minor Nazi intrusions.

As a young boy I attended a convent school, where the strict but kindly nuns made a lasting impression on me. The medium of instruction was the *Penny Catechism,* and I recall my mother patiently insisting that I memorize the answers. That catechism contains more solid theology than the shelves of glossy paperbacks that fill religious book-stores today. Then I went on to St. Joseph's College, Beulah Hill, in south London, where I was taught by the De La Salle Brothers, a French order devoted to teaching. The whole spirit of the school was thoroughly Catholic; each lesson started with a prayer and there was a religious instruction class every day. The example of these men was an inspiration. They lived incredibly hard lives, teaching unruly boys for six or more hours per day, marking our work through the evening hours, and rising at four in the morning for hours of prayer. The teaching was excellent and we were expected to work. The brothers graded every piece of classwork and homework; each week they added up the marks and ranked us in order of our total scores. The headmaster came to each class on Saturday morning and read out the list of names in order of merit. Nowadays this would be derided as elitist, but it was certainly a strong incentive to keep us working all the time.

At least four of the brothers who taught me were excellent scientists and mathematicians, and together they encouraged my love of science. I was entranced by the power and beauty and generality of the differential equations that describe so accurately the physical world. All other subjects seemed arbitrary and inexact by comparison. To every problem in mathematics or physics there was a definite, exact answer, whereas in the waffle subjects, inconclusive discussions went on forever and there seemed to be no way of reaching a conclusion.

It is this contrast that inclines many young people to reject religion, but this was not possible for me. Were we not being taught science by men who had given their lives to Christ? Before teaching us science they always said a few words about the truths of the faith and Christian living. They had obviously thought it all through for themselves and valued their faith even higher than their science. We learned that there are physical laws and moral laws. If you disregard the law of gravitation, then you get hurt. If you ignore the church's moral teaching, then you also get hurt. To live reasonably, both sets of laws must be respected. This is not a matter of emotion or of choice, but a recognition of objective reality. To criticize the church or the pope for insisting on the moral law is like criticizing a physicist for teaching the law of gravitation. It is no more possible for the church to alter the moral law than it is for the physicist to alter the law of gravitation.

There are, of course, differences between physical and moral laws. Physical laws can be subjected to accurate numerical tests, which make possible a high degree of refinement. It is, however, also possible to test moral laws simply by living by them and seeing the consequences. The experiment takes longer but is just as decisive. We have only to open the newspapers to see the results of the wholesale flouting of moral laws. By their fruits you shall know them.

These are obvious facts. No one indulges in emotional rhetoric against the law of gravitation; it is a matter of accepting reality. It is often exceedingly painful to obey moral laws, but there is nothing else to do but just put up with it. I remember that one day at school a boy was hurt and in some pain. He got little sympathy from one of the brothers who said, kindly and firmly, "You cannot stop the pain, so just ignore it and carry on!" I have found that to be very useful advice.

However well religion is taught, each person has to assimilate it, to make it his or her own. Whatever is learned must be tested against the demands of reason and of experience; is it logically coherent, does it make sense of my experiences, and can I live by it? The most fundamental question is the existence of God. I read the *Five Ways* of Aquinas and asked myself why all hydrogen atoms are the same. They must be connected in some way, by a mind that designed and made them. The other Ways show how that mind is identified with the supreme being, Almighty God.

Then we have to face the tremendous assertion that God became man in the person of Jesus Christ. That He, through whom all things were made (in the words of the Nicene Creed) actually walked this earth of ours and was fully man. This we accept on faith, a free gift of God, but once accepted it makes sense of human history. The Jesus Christ of the Gospels cannot be described as just a gifted teacher; He was either what He said He was, the Son of God, or He was the most outrageous impostor in the whole of human history. The Gospels cannot be dismissed as just pious stories. They ring true at the deepest level, and have inspired the lives of countless millions for two millennia.

It is not possible to be a Christian without a sense of history, and the history of the church is profoundly instructive. Again and again, the church has been threatened by mortal dangers, from Gnosticism, from Manicheism, from Arianism, and from monotheism (in the anti-trinitarian sense). As Chesterton has remarked,

> "To have fallen into any of those open traps of error and exaggeration which fashion after fashion and sect after sect set along the historic path of Christendom—that would indeed have been simple. It is always simple to fall; there is an infinity of angles at which one falls, only one at which one stands. To have fallen into any one of the fads from Gnosticism to Christian Science would indeed have been obvious and tame. But to have avoided them all has been one whirling adventure; and in my vision the heavenly chariot flies thundering through the ages, the dull heresies sprawling and prostrate, the wild truth reeling but erect."[2]

In every age scandals have rocked the church and there is evidence of dissolution and decay. If it were of human origin the church would have disappeared ages ago along with all the dull heresies that seemed at the time to be mortal foes. But always, along with the decay of hallowed institutions, the ossification of ancient structures, one can see the green shoots of renewed life. As some older religious orders dwindle, new ones, austere and dedicated like Opus Dei and the Legionnaires of Christ, arise to take their place.

These are times of great trial for the church. In the wake of the Vatican Council there are strong pressures in the name of democracy and keeping up with the times for a radical reorganization of the church and a wholesale relaxation of discipline. Instead of resolutely tackling the multitude of evils inside and outside the church, attempts are made to reopen questions that have been definitively settled. It has been forgotten that the church is not a democracy. When Christ asked the apostles, "Whom do you say that I am?", Simon Peter spoke on their behalf and said, "You are the Christ, the Son of the living God." Christ then gave him the name Peter, meaning rock, and said that on this rock He will build His Church. He gave the keys of the kingdom to Peter and told him that whatever he bound on earth would be bound also in heaven and whatever he loosed on earth would be loosed also in heaven (Matt. 16:15–19; Mark 3:16; John 1:42). The image of binding and loosing signifies teaching as well as disciplinary authority.

There is rich symbolism in a key: it may have a curious shape but it has one essential virtue: it opens the door.[3] Peter is always listed first among the apostles; he is their spokesman; he was the first to enter the tomb; he was the first to meet the risen Christ; and he is called; "the first" of the apostles (Matt. 10:2). He was the first to preach to the Gentiles and received the first Gentile converts (Acts 10:34–48, 15:7–11). Thus the responsibility of governing the church is given to one man acting as the representative of Christ, and he alone has the grace of God and the power to exercise that awesome responsibility. Such power can only be given and guaranteed by God alone. Recognition and acceptance of this simple fact would save much fruitless controversy. At the present time we are greatly blessed by having a strong pope who fearlessly preaches the truth and governs the church.

The moral teaching of the church is true to life itself. As Chesterton has pointed out, the church is not only right when the world is right but, more significantly, it is right when the world is wrong. Inevitably, if the church is to remain true to Christ, it has to set its face against the world. It would have been easy, humanly speaking, for Pope Julius I to silence Athanasius and to keep the Arian East within the church; it would have been easy for Pope Clement VII to bless Henry's second marriage and thus apparently to save England for the faith. It is easy to take a soft line, to gain easy popularity, by gradually relaxing the moral law in the name of compassion. We see the results all around us: promiscuous behavior before marriage is tolerated, infidelity applauded, chastity ridiculed, unnatural vice encouraged, and innocent children by the million murdered by the medical profession. Only the Catholic and the Orthodox Churches have refused to compromise.

These are some of the reasons why, by the grace of God, I have retained my faith. It is of course easy to be a skeptic, to demolish other people's beliefs and don the mantle of academic impartiality. But we are not disembodied intellects; we live in the real world and have to make decisions every day. How can we make them without definite beliefs and a rule of life that has been tested against reason and experience? Indeed, science itself is based on very special beliefs about the natural world, beliefs not found in other cultures. Further examination shows that they are Christian beliefs, and this is why science as we know it achieved its only viable birth in western Europe in the High Middle Ages.[4]

After leaving St. Joseph's College, I went to Imperial College, University of London, to study physics, and after graduation stayed on to do research under the supervision of Sir George Thomson. Then followed a period at University College London with Sir Harrie Massey, about a year as a Lecturer in Physics at the University of Reading, and then to Oxford where I have remained.

Most of that time I have spent learning and teaching physics, and on research into nuclear physics. It has proved a deeply satisfying activity, one that can easily absorb all the time available. It is, however, not possible for a Christian to ignore the wider effects of science and technology. Scientific research into nuclear physics, originally undertaken purely out of desire to find out about the innermost structure of the material world, has had great and unexpected impact on world history. The most spectacular instance of this is the atomic bomb that brought World War II to a sudden end. The scientists responsible for developing the atomic bomb were totally absorbed in their task, but as soon as the war ended they began to think about their responsibilities. It was clear to them that the pattern of international relations had been irrevocably altered, so that war between the great powers was so unimaginably dangerous that every effort must be made to make it impossible. Furthermore, the development of the nuclear reactor had provided a new source of power that could be of the greatest benefit to mankind. These applications of nuclear physics for evil and for good were not understood by the politicians responsible for decisions in the post-war world, and still less by the general public. There was clearly a great work of education to be undertaken, and the nuclear physicists were the only ones who could do it. The scientists at Los Alamos wrote articles, gave public lectures, and founded the Federation of Atomic Scientists in order to educate the public.

In Britain leading scientists formed the Atomic Scientists' Association for the same purpose. The scientists at Imperial College were particularly active and as a young graduate student in the late 1940s I was drawn into these activities; soon I was a member of the Council and editor of the *Atomic Scientists' Journal*. At that time the public was very receptive and there were many articles looking forward to the nuclear age. Then a new generation of science journalists arose and took over the work, so that the scientists gradually felt that their work was done and they could return to their laboratories. The Atomic Scientists' Association was wound up, and those who were still active found a new outlet for their work in the newly-founded Pugwash movement. The motivation behind this movement is that "An ever-growing number of scientists now realise that they have to share the responsibility of governments to utilise knowledge for constructive purposes, so that beyond the interests of individual groups and countries the achievements of science and technology shall benefit the welfare of mankind as a whole and not contribute to its detriment." It was originally concerned mainly with the problem of disarmament, but over the years its concern has widened to include the whole field of science and public affairs.

Many discussions during my student days showed that there is another area where the scientist has a particular responsibility. There is a widespread impression that science has rendered traditional religion obsolete. It is believed that science and technology can now provide the answers to age-old problems previously considered to be the concern of religion. When we are ill, we call in the doctor, and we no longer consider it sensible to pray for rain, or indeed for anything else. The prestige of science greatly impresses young people, and they drift away from Christianity. This is a problem that can only be tackled convincingly by Christians with scientific training. It is, however, by no means easy. It requires not only a knowledge of science, but also of theology, together with the history and philosophy of science. Fortunately, the Newman Association provided a series of lectures on theology, philosophy, and the philosophy of science given by the Jesuits of Heythrop College, and I was able to attend some of these courses when a graduate student in London. I also founded the Newman Association Philosophy of Science Group for Catholics who wanted to study such problems, and edited its *Bulletin*. At one time there were several hundred members, but after I left London it gradually faded away. These activities certainly took much of my time, and probably retarded my career, but they gave me a wider perspective of science and its place in human society.

During my early Oxford years, I was mostly occupied with research and teaching, and by the responsibilities of a young family. I retained my interest in the relations of theology to science, and was fortunate to meet Fr. Stanley L. Jaki, a Hungarian Benedictine priest with doctorates in systematic theology and in nuclear physics. Over the years he has written a series of scholarly books covering every aspect of the subject, and they constitute a sound perspective and an inexhaustible mine of information. At the present time there is great and growing interest in the relation between religion and science. Groups in many countries like the Science and Religion Forum in the United Kingdom and the European Society for the Study of Science and Theology arrange conferences and publish periodicals. The John Templeton Foundation has greatly assisted these activities by sponsoring lectures, courses, and meetings.

It is a great privilege to be able to spend one's life in a university, pursuing research and teaching, without having to worry unduly about the necessities of life. Despite much lip service to the contrary, professional advancement depends almost entirely on research, so there is a temptation to skimp one's teaching. Experience shows, however, that conscientious teaching is richly rewarding, and sometimes contributes ideas useful to research. The activity of research is a cooperative endeavor and we learn from each other. Over the years I have been able to make many friends worldwide through research, and I greatly value these connections.

Another area of activity started when I was introduced to Nicholas Zernov, the founder of the Orthodox community in Oxford. His gentle courtesy and obvious saintliness concealed a steely devotion to the church and he lost no opportunity to further his plans. Sometime after our first meeting, I received an invitation to tea with him and his wife Melitza. Knowing his ways, I wondered what minor task he had in mind for me, and was astonished when he invited me to become chairman of the council of the Orthodox House in Oxford. Thus began a long and greatly valued association with the Orthodox Church. Through my Orthodox friends I have come to know their deep spirituality and strong faith. I particularly recall a visit to Mount Athos, home of a vigorous and austere monasticism. The Orthodox have retained a sense of sacred mystery that is so often lacking among Catholics. We have so much to learn from each other, and our beliefs on the fundamentals of the faith are almost identical. Our communion indeed is so profound that it lacks little to attain the fullness that would permit a common celebration of the Lord's Eucharist.[5] The original separation came about very largely for political reasons and its continuation is agonizingly painful. We must pray that full union will be soon reestablished.

One frequently hears talk about the role of chance in our lives: "I had a lucky escape"; "I met him quite by chance"; "evolution took place by chance"; and so on, as if chance is a causative agent. This way of thinking has apparently received support from modern physics. Thus Heisenberg's uncertainty principle is taken to mean that the microworld is inherently fuzzy and governed by chance, and indeed Heisenberg went so far as to say that the law of causality had been definitely disproved. Further arguments for the indeterminacy of the world are based on chaos theory. This is all profoundly mistaken; when we speak of chance we mean that so far we do not know the cause. This misinterpretation of quantum mechanics comes from the unjustified assumption that quantum mechanics applies to each individual system. On the contrary, it is an essentially statistical theory that enables us to predict the average behavior of an ensemble of similar systems. In this perspective the so-called quantum paradoxes vanish, while leaving intact the possibility of a fully determined microworld. This is indeed what we expect for a world created by God and given by Him the properties that exactly determine its behavior. Here we are speaking only of the natural world; we have free will and are not wholly part of the natural world. Our lives are not governed by chance; whatever happens to us is known to God and permitted by Him.

From time to time in life one is confronted with opportunities and decisions, hopes and desires. It is natural to pray for what we want, and we are told that prayer is always answered. I have found this to be profoundly true, and the answer is generally no. With the passing of time it then becomes apparent that "no" was the right answer. To have given me what I wanted would have been a disaster. God moulds our lives far more surely than we can. He speaks to us by the actions of those around us, and sometimes even through people who intend to harm us. It is better to relax and take things as they come, not seeking to see the distant scene, and treating those two impostors, triumph and disaster, just the same. Newman said it all:

> God has created me to do Him some definite service; He has committed some work to me which He has not committed to another. I have my mission—I never may know it in this life, but I shall be told it in the next. Somehow I am necessary for His purposes. I have a part in His great work; I am a link in a chain, a bond of connexion between persons. He has not created me for naught. I shall do good, I shall do His work; I shall be an angel of peace, a preacher of truth in my own place, while not intending it, if I do but keep His commandments and serve Him in my calling.
>
> Therefore I will trust Him. Whatever, wherever I am, I can never be thrown away. If I am in sickness, my sickness may serve Him; in perplexity, my perplexity may serve Him; if I am in sorrow, my sorrow may serve Him. My sickness, or perplexity, or sorrow may be the necessary causes of some great end, which is quite beyond us. He does nothing in vain; He may prolong my life, He may shorten it; He knows what He is about. He may take away my friends, He may throw me among strangers, He may make me feel desolate, make my spirits sink, hide the future from me—still He knows what He is about.[6]

References

1. Eamon Duffy, *The Stipping of the Altars* (New Haven: Yale University Press, 1992).
2. G. K. Chesterton, *Orthodoxy* (London: Unicorn Books, 1939).
3. Stanley L. Jaki, *The Keys of the Kingdom* (Chicago: The Franciscan Herald Press, 1986).
4. Peter E. Hodgson, "The Christian Origin of Science" (Coyne Lecture in Cracow, Poland, 1995).
5. The *Catechism* of the Catholic Church (London: Geoffrey Chapman, 1994), 838.
6. John Henry Cardinal Newman, *Meditations and Devotions* (London: Longmans Green and Co., 1893).

6

COSMIC RAYS AND

WATER SPIDERS

STANLEY L. JAKI

Society makes strange claims on many of us. It expects politicians to be upright, reporters to be truthful, businessmen to be honest, clergymen to be virtuous, and scientists to be men of universal wisdom. Those who have spent much of their lives in studying science and religion are often expected to do the impossible: to prove religion from science. It cannot be done, and certainly not when the religion to be proven is left carefully undefined. It never pays to try to firm up a patch of cloud. But to say this is rather risky at a time when "playing church" has become the hallmark of having "mature" religion, though not something authoritatively definite about maturity. No wonder that even the One who claimed to himself all authority under heaven and earth is subordinated to the authority of a "higher criticism" whose champions cannot see higher than themselves.

In speaking about science there is less risk of being trapped in fog-mongering. The reason is simple. On more than one occasion prominent physicists have come up with pithy phrases that go to the very essence of exact science, physics, the very ideal which cultivators of other branches of science try to emulate, with more or less success. One such phrase is Hertz's dictum: "Maxwell's theory is Maxwell's system of equations."[1] For those who find this too esoteric, there is Eddington's warning that science, by which he meant physics, "cannot handle even the multiplication table singlehanded."[2] Both these phrases should reveal that in any branch of science the amount of fog should be inversely proportional to the mathematics, or quantitative precision, it embodies. This precision, quantitative precision, makes talking about science relatively risk free.

But nothing is so risky or mistaken as to try to perorate on that basis about anything else, including religion. Why then should one who is trained as a physicist and a theologian, and has studied all his life the relation of science and religion, be expected to prove religion from science? Is it not to ask him to throw caution to the wind? Why expect him to regard religion, usually left unspecified, with the kind of precision it cannot have even when properly defined?

Thus, even if one leaves, for the moment, religion unspecified, it would still be true that if a religion (or its theology) has no foundation of its own to stand on, it does not deserve to be propped up, even by science. Indeed, many years of study and reflection lead me to think that, concerning the relation of science and religion, there is good reason to begin with a kind of shock treatment, which, for some time, I have grown fond of formulating with a touch of irreverence: "What God has separated no man should join together." By joining, which is man's work, I mean fusing and ultimately confusing. As to the separation, which I think is God's work, I mean simply this: The cleavage between the metric and the non-metric, that is, what is measurable and not measurable, cannot be bridged conceptually.

The metric, or measurable, properties of anything are the basic and sole business of science, the very point implied in Hertz's dictum. Religion, in turn, deals with issues that are imponderable in the sense that they cannot be measured by calipers, etalons, or any of the marvelous devices science has produced in stunning variety. There is no opposition between being a virtuous man and also six feet tall, but of these two properties only physical height can be measured. A person's virtuousness can be put in the scales, but the resulting measure is very different from the one which science can provide. Unless this difference is kept in focus from the very start, while discoursing on the relation of science and religion, all that discourse will turn into an effort to firm up a patch of fog.

This is not to suggest that sharp focusing on this point has been an overriding concern for me ever since I started writing on the subject of science and religion. Origins have a way of hiding themselves even in the light of keen retrospect. But very clear in my memory are two details from my student years that may serve as a starting point in sketching my journey toward that irreverent shock treatment, although they may by themselves indicate a very different direction.

I knew at the age of seven that I wanted to become a priest. I never had a serious doubt on that score, either before or after I was ordained a priest as a member of the Benedictine Order. By the time I was sixteen I knew that I wanted to be a theologian too. My mind, however, was driven in two other directions as well. One was history. Then as now I feel dissatisfied with my grasp of any point as long as its history is hidden from me. Many years later I found that perhaps the most incisive interpreter of exact science in modern times, Pierre Duhem (1861–1916), also felt this way. His monumental work is a proof that such is not a useless concern. In addition, the kind of curiosity that propels scientific interest has also been very strong with me from early youth. Thus at the age of twelve, I slipped into a lecture hall, where I was the only one below thirty or so, to hear a talk on cosmic rays. I gained the impression that I understood everything. If I grasped anything at all, the credit should go to the lecturer, a Benedictine priest, who for eight years taught me mathematics in the gymnasium (an exacting form of middle school) in my native town, Győr, Hungary. I did not suspect then that twenty years later I would do, in another part of the world, my doctoral research on physics under the mentorship of Dr. Victor F. Hess, the Nobel laureate discoverer of cosmic rays. Anyone thrilled by cosmic rays cannot help being intrigued by the cosmos. Not a small part of my work in the history and philosophy of science turned out to be about the stellar universe.

Five years after that lecture on cosmic rays, the same Benedictine father, who also taught apologetics to seniors in the same gymnasium, asked me to read aloud to the class a passage about water spiders from a book whose title I cannot remember. But few things stand out so vividly in my memory as that passage. Almost fifty years later my heart leapt for joy, as if carried back into my distant younger years, when I found in a book, *Biology for Everyman*, by J. Arthur Thomson, the following lines, so reminiscent of that passage in Hungarian:

> The water-spider *(argyroneta natans)* which spends most of its life under water, makes a tent of silk on the floor of the pool, mooring it to stones and the like by silk threads like tent-ropes. Sometimes the shelter is woven among water-weeds. If the tent is on the floor of the pool it is flat to begin with, but the spider proceeds to buoy it up with air. Helped by a special thread, fixed at the bottom and to water-weeds at the surface, the spider ascends and entangles air in the hairs of the body. Climbing down the rope, like a drop of quick-silver because of the air bubbles, it passes under the silken sheet and presses off the air. The air is caught by the silk sheet, and after many journeys the nest becomes like a dome or diving bell, full of dry air. In this remarkable chamber, dry though under water, the mother-spider lays her eggs, and there her offspring are hatched out. The dry dome may be used as a shelter during the winter, when the spider remains inactive. . . .[3]

The memory of that passage never faded in my mind as the subject of evolution gradually became a consuming interest for me, mainly because failure to understand it properly is devouring so many minds who deserve better. The evolutionary lore has acted as a major roadblock against speaking intelligently about science and religion. This happened not only because agnosticism and materialism have been foisted on Darwinism from its very inception, but also because some have tried to cast evolution into a scenario of ever ascending spiritual self-perfection. Long before Teilhard de Chardin came up with his profuse diction about an Omega Point unsupported with sedulous elaborations about the Alpha Point, similar scenarios appeared at regular intervals from almost the moment that saw the several thousand copies of the first edition of *The Origin of Species* snapped up within a few hours.

In view of my emphasis on the radical conceptual difference between the metric and the nonmetric, it becomes a foregone conclusion that there can be no such scenario. Such is one of the principal conclusions that gradually became crystallized in my mind during more than fifty years of intense interest in and systematic study of the two fields, science and religion.

Another conclusion may appear positive, but only to those who have a positive appreciation of a philosophy that can stand on its own feet, without begging for handouts from science, and what is worse, from scientists who often know next to nothing about philosophy. This can be the case even when a scientist, like Einstein, has a gut feeling for reality as existing independently of man's thinking about it. When no such gut feeling is on hand, as was the case with Niels Bohr, the outcome is simply pathetic both in itself and in its destructive seductiveness. Witness the conceptual orgy, dressed in the most esoteric scientific technicalities, within which the wave function for the universe is made to collapse by conscious thought, although no such learned minds have ever tried to do the same with the wave function of a gold bar, and not even with that of a club sandwich.

To know that hungry pigs will not fatten by dreaming about heaps of acorns is worth more philosophically than shelves of books whose authors become entangled ever more desperately in the logical fallacies of the starting point of the Copenhagen philosophy of quantum mechanics. One needs philosophy, not science, to see beyond the surface where science unfolds more and more of the enormous degree of specificity of the material universe. Specificity is suchness. It is the registering of suchness that sparks inquiry after causes: why such and not something else? Of course, one need not be a scientist to see suchness everywhere where there is knowledge and inquiry. But the suchness revealed by modern science about every aspect of the living and the nonliving is simply astonishing. Suffice to think of the double helix of DNA molecules and of the properties of quarks, which are strictly quantitative, although denoted as flavors and colors. Such specificities, of which libraries can be filled, have a philosophical significance, which a theologian can ignore only at his enormous disadvantage in this age of science.

I do not mean the theologian whose God is the precipitate of process theology, adored in Sunday swim-ins, and savored by chewing nuts, cheese, dates, and gulping down glasses of port. True mysticism never goes without a high degree of self-imposed deprivation. In the absence of this, one can at best *talk* of mysticism and even of religion; in disregard of the injunction that one must be a doer of the word of

God and not merely a listener to it, let alone an uninterested listener. By theologian I mean the one, learned or not, whose God is the Father in heaven who in turn has to be begged for the daily bread, for the forgiveness of one's sins, for escape from temptations, because He is that only Father who is truly Almighty. The term "Almighty" means, however, that he is the Maker of heaven and earth, or of that All which is the Universe, writ large. The Son logically belongs here as the "Savior of Science," the very title of a book of mine that came fairly late, but perhaps not too late, in my meditations on science and religion. There is nothing wrong with that as long as evolution means maturation and not the pulling of a rabbit out of a hat by, say, giant mutations. Such giants, no more real than the seven dwarfs, belong neither to the genesis of theology nor to the science of genetics.

In fact, the Son should be brought in now, however briefly, because the Father created everything in his Word, the Logos. Such is the reason why the Universe has to be fully logical. Were historians of science, so eager to pinpoint trivial starting points, appreciative of the fact that not the Greeks, but Saint Athanasius, so terribly otherworldly for them, formulated in his struggle against the Arians the full rationality of the material universe, a good deal of the alleged opposition between science and religion would vanish like the morning fog. Of course, some theologians too, busy with the relation of science and religion, should do some soul searching. I mean those who inherited a dislike for the Athanasian, or rather Nicean dogma of the Word's consubstantiality just because the word *consubstantial* cannot be found in the Bible. Yet the Bible certainly teaches that the Father created everything in the Son. Such a Son has to be strictly divine, because even Almighty God cannot subdelegate his power to create to a mere creature, however exalted.

First, therefore, the createdness of the universe. Recognition of this is the very minimum without which there can be no religion that includes prayer to a personal Creator. If the theologian is learned and logical (unfortunately these two qualifications need no longer go together), he must assert that reason may safely infer the existence of the Creator. Science can help him greatly, provided he knows what is being done when one infers the reality of something unseen. The word *inference* is crucial, because all human knowledge that relates not to realities directly experienced on the ground floor, points to levels higher up, to realities grasped by climbing mentally, that is, by inferences, to the second floor and to floors even higher. Knowledge is a seven-story mountain, with the number seven symbolizing that perfection that goes with any sound inferential grasp of the existence of God.

So much for the assertion that much of our knowledge (even in science) is an inferential knowledge and is such long before God, the ultimate, becomes the object of one's reasoned inference. If this is not kept in mind and one's feet are not kept on the ground floor, or the first floor where data are gathered for higher inferences, one will be overawed by claims of modern cosmologists that their expertise enables them to create entire universes literally out of nothing. Clearly then one can play not only church but one can play God as well. Such is the acme of the new reformation, achieved by a drastic abuse of science.

Hapless thinking about quantum mechanics merely put the icing on a cake that began to be baked two hundred years ago by perhaps the most consummate chameleon in the history of science. I mean Laplace, who kept conveniently changing in order to remain on the crest of the wave as Monarchy turned into Convention, Convention into Terror, Terror into Directorate, Directorate into Empire, Empire into Restoration. I hope and pray that the report about his repentance on his deathbed is true. There is no more sound reason for believing in God than that he is infinitely merciful. This, however, presupposes that one first dissociates oneself from that modern mankind that takes man's fallen condition for his healthy state so that one may glory shamelessly in one's very shame.

Laplace's famous words, "I do not need that hypothesis," may express either sound science, or something utterly unsound, philosophically that is. Two hundred years ago Laplace sold the idea that our present, exceedingly specific physical world evolved from a nondescript or nebulous primordial cloud, about which he knew only that it was very nebulous indeed. When in 1801 Laplace uttered these words, he did not yet feel the social need to profess belief in God. However, he did not have to be a philosopher to sense that an emphatically nebulous entity never calls for questions about its nebulosity, precisely because it verges on the nondescript. If the supposedly original entity, a cosmic nebula, is nondescript, it automatically parades as that ultimate entity about which no further questions are asked. Such is the pseudoscientific death knell delivered by pantheism to natural theology.

The implicitness of Laplace's "atheistic" or rather "pantheistic" reasoning was eventually made explicit by Herbert Spencer, who spun philosophical fairy tales about the evolution of the non-homogeneous from the primordially homogeneous. As was noted above, inquiry, curiosity, search for causes are sparked by the registering of suchness or specificities. Now if the primordial state is imagined to be utterly homogeneous (nebulous) then it will not prompt one to raise the question why such and not something else, because what is allegedly absolutely homogeneous has no suchness. It therefore begins to pose as the ultimate in intelligibility and being. Such is, in a nutshell, the logic of modern scientistic materialism and atheism. There is no opposing it unless one goes to the basics of epistemology. Without doing so one cannot counter the icing on the cosmic cake, which is busily baked by some luminaries of quantum cosmology.

What these should say is rather that modern scientific cosmology shows across space and time a universe that cannot be more different from the universe that originated from a primordial nondescript state. Whatever is observed by science about physical reality, whether about its present or remote stage, it is specificity. The philosophically sensitive theologian can and must utilize these results of science to strengthen his inference about the existence of a Creator. But he should be on guard, lest he assume that science will do this for him. Science, which "cannot handle even the multiplication table singlehanded," cannot say a word about causality, not even about things real, and nor can it prove that there is a strict totality of things, or a Universe. Science, including Einsteinian cosmology, cannot do this for a very simple reason: the truths of science demand experimental verification. But no scientist, no scientific instrument, can be carried beyond the universe to observe and thereby scientifically verify it. The verification of the universe is an eminently philosophical task.

This task can be achieved, as I argued in my Forwood Lectures given at the University of Liverpool in 1992, available as *Is there a Universe?*[4] Youthful but genuine enthusiasm about cosmic rays had to issue in a resolve to fathom the grounds that justify the strict use of the word *universe* or *cosmos*. Three years earlier, in my Farmington Institute (Oxford) Lectures, *God and the Cosmologists,* I had already developed this new form of the cosmological argument.[5] It must, however, have been clearly set forth in earlier works of mine, such as the Gifford Lectures, *The Road of Science and the Ways to God,*[6] or else the citation for the Templeton Prize for 1987 would not have mentioned it as one of the reasons why that prize was awarded to me.

Another reason was my investigation of the basic framework within which the relation of science and religion can be meaningfully dealt with. The principal aspect of that framework is the unique standing of the category of quantities among all the other categories of thought as listed by Aristotle in the *Categories.* I refer to Aristotle with some trepidation, because of the prejudice that a point made over two millennia ago, especially if made by him, cannot be true. In fact, in a sense, much of the modern philosophical agenda is aimed at showing that qualities, action, passion, substance accidents, etc., can be reduced to quantities. Such is a chief contention of the Hegelian right and left. Logical positivists claim much the same when they restrict meaning to statements that can be handled in the manner of mathematics. Hence the formalism of symbolic logic, which, incidentally, cannot even prove the reality of a book, filled with symbols, strangely resembling those of mathematical operators.

Here again it was only in recent years that this difference between quantities and all other categories has taken, in my thinking about religion and science, a central place. I wonder what those engineers of optical instrumentation thought of my paper, read at their vast annual meeting in Orlando, Florida, on April 14, 1996, under the title: "Words: Blocks, Amoebas, or Patches of Fog? Artificial Intelligence and the Foundations of Fuzzy Logic."[7] But unless promoters of artificial intelligence machines consider that difference, they will never understand why their blueprints of thinking machines will forever remain very fuzzy indeed.

This point was explicitly made already in the fifth chapter, "Language, Logic, Logos," added to the second edition (1989) of my *Brain, Mind, and Computers,* whose first edition (1969) received the Lecomte du Nouy Prize. I do not know whether this point was among those which the author of *Gödel, Escher and Bach,* who cast there an emotion-laden vote on behalf of artificial intelligence, had in mind when he wrote in his book that I had made some points worth pondering. He never went on record by pondering them, even as much as by listing them. Such is the new scholarship: mere reference to a problem, without even naming it, passes for its successful resolution. There was no real reply to *Brain, Mind, and Computers,* although none other than Herbert Feigl voiced the need for it. Apparently I said something very important there that cannot be attacked except with a boomerang.

Professor Feigl, then as later, was one of those very rare academics who never tried to brush off scholarship just because it went together with an ideology diametrically opposite to his. Such was his reaction to the typescript of my first major book on science and religion, *The Relevance of Physics* (1966), which he read for the University of Chicago Press. That book contains passages that anticipate those later observations of mine about the strange limitedness of quantitative notions. The broader meaning of the point is, of course, that science is largely irrelevant about most of what human cogitation is about. This has to be clearly realized if one is to speak meaningfully about the relation of science and religion, instead of serving up indigestible dreams about the two being fused together or standing in radical opposition to one another. They are merely different and will forever remain so, mental acrobatics notwithstanding.

Herein lay another reason for me to find in Duhem a very germane soul and mind. Had Duhem achieved nothing except unearthing through heroic research the medieval (and distinctly Christian) origin of modern science he would have already immortalized his name in the genuine annals of the historiography of science. Duhem was also the foremost among the sane philosophical interpreters of physics, in addition to being a first-rate theoretical physicist. I first came across his towering intellect and noble character when a short biography of him, written by his daughter, fell into my hands. Well, if not even a sparrow falls to the ground without our heavenly Father willing it, He must have something to do with the moments and places when this or that book falls into one's hands. And just in time, because shortly afterwards I heard one of the chief luminaries among still living historians of science dismiss interest in medieval science as a hobby of Roman Catholics, and especially of priests, such as Duhem. He choked when I told him, in the presence of quite a few, that a chief source on Duhem's life is a book written by his only child, a daughter.

Shortly afterwards (around 1961) I read the second edition of Duhem's *La théorie physique* (1914), available also in an English translation as *The Aim and Structure of Physical Theory*. One of the two additions to that second edition is what may be Duhem's finest essay, "The Physics of a Believer." There Duhem begins by answering the charge of a critic (Abel Rey) of the first edition (1906), that his philosophy is "that of a believer." "Of course"—Duhem writes in reply and rebuttal—"I believe with all my soul in the truth that God has revealed to us and that He has taught us through His Church. I have never concealed my faith, and I hope from the bottom of my heart that He in whom I hold it shall keep me from ever being ashamed of that faith: in this sense it is permissible to say that the physics I profess is the physics of a believer."[8]

As a Roman Catholic philosopher and historian of science, mainly of physics, astronomy, and cosmology, I could have never put it remotely as well as Duhem did. And I could continue with Duhem, who noted right there and then, that it was not in that sense that his critic labeled his physics "the physics of a believer." That critic, for whom it was inconceivable that there could be an epistemology between the extremes of empiricism (positivism) and idealism, charged Duhem with injecting religion into physics, precisely because he proceeded between those extremes, or rather mental abysses. It shows something of the darkness dominating secular academia around the turn of the century, that realist metaphysics, the epistemological middle road taken by Duhem, could be taken for mysticism and therefore for religion. In the same way some of my critics, unable to see that middle ground, and just as blind therefore to some salient facts of the history of science, have grown fond of dismissing my work as that of a Catholic. This blindness they have inherited as a staple feature of post-Enlightenment western culture, steeped in contempt for the Middle Ages. In fomenting this contempt, often growing into hatred, the heirs of the Reformation have become strange bedfellows with Voltaire, Diderot, Hume,

Gibbon, and the rest. For these two camps, though for very different reasons, nothing was so vital as to paint the Middle Ages as black as possible. A dangerous tactic, because it prevents the secular historian from seeing plain, vastly documented facts of scientific history, and prevents the Protestant scholar from seeing the inner logic of "private judgment." I would not mention this had not a prominent Protestant theologian, very busy with science, shared with me his anxiety about that logic. His words, uttered in complete privacy, still ring in my ears: "Protestantism logically leads to naturalism." Not that he said anything new with that.

Contrary to the expectations of that critic of his, Duhem became celebrated among philosophers of science, at least in the sense that they keep borrowing from him heavily, without giving him a thimbleful of credit. There is an awful amount of food for thought in the few lines of a postcard that Lakatos once sent to Feyerabend, stating that all of Popper's philosophy is a rehash of Duhem's. This is, of course, true only in the sense that Popper and others borrowed some of Duhem's method without endorsing with him that ontology (realist metaphysics) that alone assures that the method deals with reality and not merely with the calculations of the physicist and with the ideas of the philosophers of science about those calculations, which all too often they cannot follow.

In referring to that postcard Feyerabend gave the impression that he was fully aware of his indebtedness to Duhem. He might have been, but he gave no inkling of this in his printed works. Such is academic objectivity, whose practitioners can get away with conceptual murders once they occupy a prestigious chair. Equally revealing is a facet in Kuhn's philosophy of science, which the author of a doctoral dissertation on his work pointed out about twenty years ago: The principal Kuhnian theses are all in Duhem, except, of course, that irrationality that destroys Kuhn's ideas on scientific revolutions as so many drastic paradigm changes of the human mind. As a loyal son of the Catholic Church, which is continuity incarnate, Duhem would have never cavorted in radical discontinuities in religion (theology), or in philosophy, or in science. This is why among other things, of which more shortly, Duhem is an *Uneasy Genius* (1984), the title of my half-a-million-word monograph on him.[9]

I was indeed dismissed time and again as a "Catholic" historian and philosopher of science (and a Jesuit to boot, which, being a Benedictine, I am not). This should be fairly understandable. In this age, when science is corralled by any Tom, Dick and Harry in order to gain respectability for his ideas, few things can be so resented by a Protestant as two claims of mine. One, of which more later, is that creative science has always been connected with a middle-road epistemology, which is incompatible with the Ockhamism inherited by the Reformers. This is, of course, difficult to understand in this age when some Protestant theologians who divorced their field from philosophy gained high repute, for a while at least. Logic can never be exorcized forever.

The other claim, the medieval origins of modern science, is more easily resented, especially when both believing and nominally believing Protestants hang on to the idea, as if it were a lifebelt for them in this age of science, that science originated under the spiritual impact of Puritans, and perhaps with Luther and Calvin. These last two were sheer mystery mongers, the former rudely, the latter subtly, in their interpretation of Genesis 1, which even today is a touchstone of truth as to whether one is talking sense or nonsense about the relation of science and religion. Those who find this statement of mine outrageous may wish to consult my monograph, *Genesis 1 through the Ages* (1992), a history of interpretations of that first chapter of Genesis.[10] About that chapter of Genesis, a Protestant clergyman friend of mine, for many years a Navy chaplain, once sighed: if only that chapter were missing from the Bible! Although he has had that book of mine for years, he still has not brought himself to read it. Remember those who refused to look through Galileo's telescope.

Nor could the marshaling of evidence about the medieval Christian origins of science please Muslims. For them nothing is so bothersome in this age of science, that witnesses the full-scale technologization of their native lands, as are those origins. The same holds true of Hindus as well. Nehru made a laughing stock of himself in claiming that the modern scientific spirit first flourished in ancient India. As a founder of modern India, Nehru felt it had to be decorated with science too. Far more Hindu was Gandhi, who decried time and again scientific preoccupations. At any rate, during one of my Oxford lectures, a group of Muslims in the audience suddenly jumped up and shouted all sorts of invectives at me. One of them, raising his fist, excoriated my book, *Science and Creation: From Eternal Cycles to an Oscillating Universe.*[11] No wonder. The book deals with the most obvious but most studiedly ignored feature of scientific history: the repeated stillbirths of science in all great ancient cultures (all steeped in pantheism), and its only viable birth in the Christian west.

That viable birth was touched off by an indispensable spark, Buridan's formulation around 1348 of the idea of inertial movement. Now Buridan was part of that Christian west, where monotheism was Christian monotheism. In other words, the only God who was believed in was that God who sent his only begotten Son, in fact, created everything in Him. The Logos, this infinite rationality, therefore could create but a fully rational world, a point made by Athanasius in his struggle against the Arians. The latter, incidentally, have many followers nowadays among "enlightened" Christian theologians, busy rehabilitating Arius, the worst of all heresiarchs. But because the Son was "only begotten," that is, *monogenes, unigenitus,* He therefore dethroned from that rank the cosmos, the *to pan,* or the universe, which all educated ancient Greeks and Romans took for the only begotten emanation from the First Principle. So much about the theological matrix from which Buridan's spark jumped forth, in illustration of Christ's words: Seek first the kingdom of God and the rest will be given to you. For further details the reader of this essay may wish to search in a library for my book, *The Savior of Science,* for years now out of print. Cultural historians of the west still need to see that spark, first noticed by Duhem, and try to digest it. Then they must part with inherited prejudices and vested interests, including plush academic emoluments, ready access to prestigious presses, rich foundations, and the like. Why? A personal detail may not be amiss. Some months after the University of Chicago Press published my first major book, *The Relevance of Physics* (1966), I went through Chicago and paid a visit at the Press. After my visit, a big wheel there told a friend of mine on the faculty of the University of Chicago that "it is a pity that Father Jaki came here in a Roman collar." "Why?" my friend (not a Catholic) asked in disbelief. "Because," so went the explanation, "were Father Jaki to come here in a sport jacket, we would be on our knees in front of him." I have no reason to doubt the verbatim veracity of this report.

By then the typescript of that book had been rejected by six major publishers, academic and commercial. Yet no less a figure of modern physics than Walter Heitler was to write in a review in *American Scientist* that the book is a long awaited remedy to the sundry misinterpretations of physics and should be read by all physicists. Herbert Feigl, the third reader of the typescript for the Press, wrote in his report that the author displays on every page an impressive scholarship. This certainly offset the puzzlement of the second reader who did not know what to do with the book.

A year after *The Relevance* was published, its first reader wrote me a long letter, to which he attached a copy of his report to the Press. He began the letter with saying that his major problem with the typescript was not to praise it too highly. But he could not resist ending his report by citing Agrippa's words to Paul: "A little more, Paul, and you will make a Christian of me." The writer of the report disclosed to me that he, a professor of electrical engineering at a big midwestern university, was an agnostic Jew, desperately searching for the meaning of life.

In all *The Relevance* there is no pleading whatever on behalf of Jesus Christ, except perhaps a very indirect one at the end. There I quote Whitehead's phrase that only the Babe's silent birth in the manger produced in history a stir greater than science did. Why then was that professor of electrical engineering not impressed by that phrase of Whitehead, although he must have known it for years? Obviously because Whitehead, son of a Church of England clergyman, stopped believing in the Babe just when he would have needed that faith in Him most, sometime during World War I, when a son of his became one of the war's countless victims. This loss of faith transpires everywhere in Whitehead's most widely read book, *Science and the Modern World,* which contains that priceless phrase of his.

Less than a year after *The Relevance* was published, a large envelope came to me. It contained an offprint of an article from *Life* magazine, about a new California enterprise: For a payment of five thousand dollars (quite a sum in 1967), the enterprise would freeze my dead body, store it, and, by thawing it at a future time specified by me, would bring me back to life. The covering letter referred to my recently published *Relevance,* with the comment that it testifies to a highly intelligent mind. Perhaps, but those salesmen obviously did not read the book. Had they done so, they would not have contacted me. Half of *The Relevance* is about the basic irrelevance of physics, this most exact of all sciences, with respect to biology (yes, biology as dealing with the living, and not with mere molecules in motion), philosophy, theology, and basic cultural concerns. Only the other or the first half is about the restricted relevance of physics even within its own domain.

But even some very competent readers of *The Relevance* failed to grasp its message, a message striking at the heart of scientism, or the claim that the method of science is the only rational activity and whatever cannot be evaluated within its terms must be irrational, or plain bogus. Now religion, by which I emphatically do *not* mean "higher estheticism," is bunk if scientism is valid. Hence as a believer I must have a crucial interest in showing the limited validity of the method of physics, this most exact of all sciences, precisely because it is heavily exploited and abused by scientism. To unfold that limited validity is, however, valid even if made to serve religious concerns, regardless of broader cultural considerations. In showing this limited validity or relevance, I heavily relied on statements made to that effect by physicists. Of the well over a thousand citations in *The Relevance,* almost all of them are taken from physicists. Nothing is so convincing about the limited relevance of exact science than to hear it stated by physicists, old and new. The reviewer of the book in *The Atomic Scientist* had in fact to admit that "Jaki forged a powerful book." Was this an ill-disguised expression of disappointment that it was not possible to say about the book that it was a forgery? Apparently it hit some in a very sensitive spot.

And why not? Had not many scientists allowed themselves to be anointed as the pontiffs of the scientific age? Not many Nobel laureates had, on receiving word about the prize, the good sense to say something similar to the remark of my dear friend, the late Eugene Wigner.

A regiment of reporters, hungry for words of wisdom about anything from the august lips of a new scientific pontiff, were astonished on hearing him state: "The prize did not make me a man of universal wisdom."

Hardly anything was grasped about *The Relevance* by that official of the American Scientific Affiliation when at a meeting of theirs he referred to that book as one in which "you can find all of Lord Kelvin's half-baked endorsements of the ether." Those statements take up less than two pages out of the more than six hundred. They are, of course, very educational for those who see how history, including scientific history, repeats itself. The adulation of the ether (an entity with contradictory properties) is now repeated in similar homages to the quantum mechanical vacuum, so full of energy that it allegedly performs what until recently has been ascribed to Almighty God alone: creates universes literally out of nothing. Clearly, between *that* physics and a religion distinct from *higher estheticism* there can be no ceasefire, not a word of dialogue. Theologians, let alone their amateur brand, who think otherwise are hapless victims of confusion or ignorance or both, which is certainly a "winning" combination nowadays, when coated in specious references to modern physics and the fashionable philosophies poured around it as so much toxic sauce.

To what extent this dubious technique is allowed to be practiced deserves to be illustrated by a recent example. I mean the effort of the religion reporter of the British daily, *The Independent*, to smooth over the problems created for the Church of England by its openly homosexual clergymen (and bishops). To make the farce complete the effort appeared in the formerly Catholic weekly, *The Tablet* (November 16, 1996). The writer begins with the claim of some conservatives that such and other troubles were brought upon the Church of England by its ordination of women. According to the reporter the connection is far more subtle. The subtlety he borrows from the science of quantum mechanics, of which he clearly knows only some catch phrases: "The ordination of women acted on Anglican ideas of authority rather as an observation is supposed to act on a sub-atomic particle in quantum physics. What had once been a delicious cloud of probabilities was suddenly constrained to collapse into a measurable fact, of fixed position—if unknowable velocity." A typical runaway misuse of modern physics in support of ultramodernism in religion or something worse. Yet anyone who knows the difference between probability functions (mere ideas) and facts should realize that skullduggery is at work and not sophistication or subtlety.

Before parting with *The Relevance,* I should say something about the late Abdus Salam, who won the Nobel Prize in 1980 for his work in fundamental particle physics and who could have become a most competent reviewer of that book of mine. He wondered whether it made sense to waste excellent style over so many pages about what we all know, namely, that physics is always incomplete. Well, it seems that as a fundamental particle physicist he read only Chapter 4, "The Layers of Matter," and even that only in part. There I stressed the chronic elusiveness of the last layer of matter and quoted physicist after physicist, old and new, to document their belief that the last layer of matter is almost within their reach. Had he read the chapter before, he would have realized that it contained a great novelty, which many Nobel laureates do not seem to know at all. More of this shortly.

Now *The Relevance* was in a sense a misnomer, though an artful one, because at that time "relevance" was *the* word that quickly caught on with everybody. As I said before, the second half of the book was about the irrelevance of physics, and only the first half about its qualified relevance even within its own domain. There I pointed out in three successive chapters that none of the three great main types of physics (organismic, or Aristotelian; mechanistic or Newtonian; and modern or essentially mathematical) can make a claim to being the final word in physics. About the two former this is now a post-mortem statement, though its historical details are enormously instructive. The death knell on the alleged finality of modern physics was sounded when it had not even completed its first quarter of a century. I mean Gödel's presentation of his incompleteness theorems before the Vienna Academy of Sciences in 1930.

Had my studies of the history of physics not exposed me to the various foibles of great scientists, I would have found it impossible to understand how this theorem could fail to be applied immediately to that modern physics whose protagonists think of the world as a pattern in numbers. This application had to wait for a full generation until it appeared in *The Relevance*. The research that went into the writing of that book, in which only physicists, past and living, speak about physics, made it clear to me that even physicists put their trousers on one leg at a time. (Some theologians give the impression, especially when spouting scientific expressions, that they can crypto-levitate and jump into their trousers with both feet in the air.)

So I was not shocked, I merely wondered, when I had my sole encounter with Professor Murray Gell-Mann. It took place at a Nobel Conference in 1976 at Gustavus Adolphus College. There he assured an audience of about 2,000 strong that within a few months, but certainly within a few years, he would be able to outline the ultimate theory of fundamental particles and also prove that such a theory necessarily has to be the ultimate theory. As one of the panelists (the others were Victor Weiskopf, Steven Weinberg, Fred Hoyle, and Hilary Putnam), I could speak up before questions were taken from the floor. So I simply but firmly told Professor Gell-Mann that he would not succeed. He might find the ultimate theory, but he could never be sure that it was *the* ultimate theory, and much less that it was *necessarily* the ultimate.

Why not? he asked me in a tone that clearly revealed that he did not like to be disputed. Well, I said, in a stronger voice: because of Gödel's theorem. What theorem? he fired back, as if he had never heard of Gödel before. I suspect he had not. A few months later I gave a talk at Boston University on cosmology. I argued, among other things, that there can be no final and necessarily true cosmological theory, as long as Gödel's theorems are valid. After the talk somebody from the audience walked up to me saying that I merely repeated Professor Murray Gell-Mann. It was now my turn to explode: What? I asked in disbelief. Well, he said that he had just come from Chicago where he heard Professor Gell-Mann state that because of Gödel's theorems a final theory of fundamental particles cannot be constructed. I gasped and told him of my encounter with Gell-Mann a month or so earlier at Gustavus Adolphus. Then it was his turn to gasp in disbelief. The punchline to this punchy story is still to come. Weinberg, still at Harvard, returned there with Hilary Putnam, who later told me that he had to give some basic information to his colleague about Gödel's theorems of which he had not been aware before he too heard me at Gustavus Adolphus. Apparently, even Hilary Putnam failed. In Weinberg's *Dreams of a Final Theory* one would look in vain for a single reference to Gödel's theorems, although they render illusory any such dream.

My life, or rather my lifelong experience concerning the relation of religion and science, has to be told largely in references to my books. In a sense they are my life story. Ever since I started writing *The Relevance,* I have spent much of my working days, including Sundays, for which I beg pardon, in researching and writing, or rather writing and rewriting. That the art of writing is rewriting I learned when I had just started writing *The Relevance,* shortly after Churchill died. Then a big New York tabloid carried on its front page the facsimile of a passage from one of Churchill's famous wartime speeches. The passage, in neat type-written form, and perfect as such, was still heavily reworked by Churchill's hand. On seeing this (later on I learned that John Henry Newman, another great master of English, usually rewrote everything three times before sending it to the printer), I got over the psychological hurdle of not being able to write a perfect copy on the first try.

After that, writing has gradually become a sort of obsession, made endurable by the fact that the coming of word processors turned the otherwise tiresome business of rewriting into a relatively easy task, compared with the use of ballpoint pens and typewriters. I could not help recalling that Pierre Duhem had to write his 350 publications (including thirty vast books) with pen and ink, and with a right hand that for the last ten years of his life suffered from *crampe d'écrivain.* Often he had to hold fast his right hand with his left hand in order to continue writing. Lucky we, who have lived to see the coming of PCs. They greatly increased my productivity. But, having produced so many pages for a higher purpose, namely, to strengthen those who believe in a Gospel undiluted by a "higher criticism" posing as science, I will not be threatened by the disillusion that overcame Herbert Spencer in his dying days. On seeing that his friends brought to his bedside the many books he had published, he was dismayed that he had no children of his own to stand by. He certainly might have learned a great deal from C. S. Lewis's gripping account, *A Grief Observed.*

But that productivity needed a surgical intervention to become eventually possible. In late 1953, a difficult tonsillectomy deprived me of the effective use of my voice for at least ten years. I was immediately out of all teaching and preaching. Only by writing could I go on teaching, which for me is always a preaching. I say this with no apologies or embarrassment. After having spent forty years in academe, I find it to be the chief breeding place of a subspecies best called spineless vertebrates. They lack intellectual spine because they refuse to admit that they preach by teaching and researching. In fact, every teaching is a sort of plain apologetics. Apologetics is pleading. To claim that one's teaching is free of even a touch of pleading on behalf of something is to practice the art of not seeing beyond one's very nose.

I kept pleading. After publishing *The Relevance,* I published a book that was originally meant to be a chapter in it as "Physics and Psychology." It grew into *Brain, Mind, and Computers.* Once this book was out of my hair (by then my hairline was rapidly receding), I could turn to what has been sheer delight to write: monographs on the history of astronomy. All had for their "ulterior" aim the illustration of chronic blindness to the obvious. First came *The Paradox of Olbers' Paradox* (1969), the story of the strange oversight by astronomers of the physical meaning of the darkness of the night sky. Given certain assumptions, entirely valid throughout the seventeenth, eighteenth, and nineteenth centuries, that darkness should have been seen as contradicting the assumed infinity of the universe, which became a scientific as well as scientistic or materialistic dogma in the nineteenth century.

Then came *The Milky Way* (1972), whose subtitle, *An Elusive Road for Science,* is literally true. The fact is that long before Thomas Wright hit, in 1750, upon the reason for the visual appearance of the Milky Way, it should have been spelled out by Newton and others. Worse, the explanation had to be rediscovered three times during the latter half of the nineteenth century. The third monograph was *Planets and Planetarians: A History of Theories of the Origin of Planetary Systems* (1976). A very checkered history indeed, especially if one considers the blind alley into which Laplace, who should have known better, guided planetary cosmogony. The material of an additional chapter to that story is unfolding in the almost willful disregard of the Earth-Moon system in estimating the number of extraterrestrial civilizations. Once considerations about the improbability of our Earth-Moon system are fed into the Drake equation, the probability of a civilization with a technology similar to ours or higher to have evolved around any star in our Milky Way, would be not 10^4 but perhaps 10^{-4} or perhaps even less.

This is a point already adumbrated in my *God and the Cosmologists* and set forth in great detail in a paper, available on the Internet, read at the October 1996 meeting of the Pontifical Academy of Sciences on micro and macro evolution. It was that meeting that John Paul II addressed with a letter on evolution, a letter that threw the media into a tailspin of their own making. The reporter of the BBC worldwide service, who contacted me in Rome, first wanted a mere five minute interview. After twenty minutes, he became disappointed on realizing that none of the headlines of the Italian newspapers was even remotely true. In sum, the pope did not embrace Darwin, while he could hail the latest achievements in evolutionary science as distinct from Darwinian ideology, the latter having for its basic dogmas the uncreatedness of the universe, and the perishing of the soul with bodily death. Whatever the sins of the Italian press, it is hardly a virtue that the BBC did not find the very truth about what the pope said worth broadcasting.

Here belong a few words about my translation into English of three classics of the history of astronomy. First, Giordano Bruno's *Ash Wednesday Supper* (1975), for which Bruno would have deserved to be burnt by scientists, that is, by all the fledgling Copernicans, right there and then when he published it in 1584. Then came Lambert's *Cosmological Letters* (1976), which prompted its reviewer in *Scientia* (Milan) to say that its notes, almost as many pages as the book itself, would necessitate the rewriting of the history of cosmology during the seventeenth and the first half of the eighteenth century. The third was Kant's *Universal Natural History and Theory of the Heavens* (1981). Doing this gave me a particular delight. The book is only one third Kant. Equally long are my introduction and the notes added to it. They show that in speaking of science Kant was an artful poseur. The evidence may perhaps awaken those who keep Kant the philosopher in high esteem because of his alleged expertise in science. Cutting science and scientists, but above all some "scientific" philosophers to size would help create a clear atmosphere in which talk about religion might not go off, again and again, on a tangent and end in clever games with mere ideas.

Sometime before all this, actually in 1970 and 1971, I wrote *Science and Creation*, mentioned above. While the secularists groaned (plenty of them among historians of science), some religionists—among them the reviewer in the *Bulletin* of the Victoria Institute, London—were ecstatic. Certainly if one is clear-sighted enough to know that pantheism is the only logical alternative to biblical revelation culminating in Christ, nothing is so unwelcome in this scientific age as the word that pantheism was the cause of the stillbirths of science and that only a Christ-based monotheism made science experience its only live birth.

The next item I shall talk about is my Gifford Lectures, given at the University of Edinburgh in 1974–75 and 1975–76, published as *The Road of Science and the Ways to God.* (That I was invited has much to do with the interest my friend, Thomas F. Torrance, took in my writings, an interest touched off by his reading of *The Relevance.*) Giving a long title to my Gifford Lectures certainly taught me that it does not easily stick, however true to the content of the book. I should have perhaps called it "Science and the Ultimate" and it still would have remained true to its real thrust. I argued in those twenty lectures that a scientist's or a philosopher's choice of the ultimate in intelligibility and being determines his dicta on science, for better or for worse. Further, one can choose God as the ultimate only if one's epistemology permits the cosmological argument, an argument very different from Kant's distortions of it, couched partly in his inept references to science. It was only fifteen years later that I had the opportunity to argue in detail, in the course of my Forwood Lectures at the University of Liverpool, that while science is unable to prove the reality of the universe, philosophy, and philosophy alone, can do it. Such is the gist of that series of lectures, *Is there a Universe?* Therefore scientific cosmologists should rename their subject matter as supergalactology or something. Such was at least the inference drawn by a prominent British astronomer who read the book. Most other astronomers still have to discover that they gently cheat in writing books on cosmology.

The Templeton Prize of 1987 had something to do with that invitation to Liverpool. Before that the Stillman Chair at Harvard could have been mine for the asking. I declined. I stuck with my university, Seton Hall, simply because I do not think that Catholic priests should abandon Catholic universities for places more prestigious in the eyes of the world. A Catholic priest should not lose sight of the biblical warning that a man of God must be on guard against abandoning the lean in favor of the fat. Such a hint is hardly to the liking of liberal Catholic intellectuals.

Whatever my failures to live up to the ideals of the priesthood, I have perhaps explicitly served it through this or that book of mine. The Gifford Lectures prompted the conversion to Catholicism of a prominent midwestern industrialist. Many others wrote about the spiritual profit they derived from it. The Church was directly the object of three books of mine. The first, *Les tendances nouvelles de l'ecclésiologie*, grew out of my doctoral dissertation. It was reprinted during Vatican II. *And on this Rock*, out in its third enlarged edition, is about a rock in Caesarea Philippi, about the word *rock* in the Old and New Testament, and about the unfailing preaching by the papacy of Jesus' divinity. *The Keys of the Kingdom* takes its starting point from the history of key-making. Science, if properly used, can be of great assistance in building a theological argument, even in biblical theology.

This is further illustrated by two other books of mine. One, *Genesis 1 through the Ages,* has already been mentioned, though not the fact that the first chapter of the Bible is also its most misinterpreted chapter. I would not have written that book, had I not surmised that the explanation that does justice both to Bible and science must be sought in reference to the sabbath observance. This point is now explicitly treated at some length in my essay, "The Sabbath Rest of the Maker of All," in the *Asbury Journal of Theology*.[12] The other book to be mentioned is *Bible and Science*.[13] The science in question is not archeology, but hard physical science. I argue there, among other things, that one's reading of the Bible should first be disentangled from the false opposition between the Hebrew and Greek mind if one is to grasp the biblical authors' commonsense perception of reality. This plainly epistemological point (any attempted refutation of which implies implicit trust in such a perception) bears heavily on the trustworthiness of the biblical authors' reports on miracles. The same holds true of any plain witness about miraculous events, such as the cures at Lourdes. As I argued in my little book, *Miracles and Physics* (1990), nothing is more mistaken than to invoke Heisenberg's uncertainty principle as if it provided a chance for God to do something physical without interfering with the laws of physics. The theologian who is still interested in free will will make an equally great mistake when he tries to defend it with a reliance on quantum mechanics. A long essay of mine, "Determinism and Reality" (1990) will make all this clear.[14]

Following the Gifford Lectures, I had the honor to give in 1977 the Fremantle Lectures at Balliol College in Oxford. They appeared as *The Origin of Science and the Science of its Origin*. It is an analysis of theories on the origin of science from Bacon on to the present. It should be read as a companion volume to *Science and Creation* and the Gifford Lectures. It was at about that time, or shortly before it, that I was elected a permanent Visiting Fellow at Corpus Christi College. By then I had become a good friend of Dr. Peter Hodgson, at Corpus, a friendship that time and distance have not weakened.

It was he who called the attention of the Farmington Institute of Oxford to my work. This resulted in two series of lectures, given in 1988 and 1989, respectively. The former came out as *God and the Cosmologists* (1989), the latter as *The Purpose of it All* (1990), both in collaboration with Scottish Academic Press, whose director, Dr. Douglas Grant, has shown an unflagging interest in my work ever since he published *Science and Creation.*

In my history of fighting the good fight on behalf of good science and true religion, I should not forget my encounter with Mr. Chauncey Stillman and the Wethersfield Institute he founded. This Institute sponsored the series of lectures that came out as *The Savior of Science* (1988). There I gave a full-bodied treatment to the theses, already mentioned above, that a monotheism steeped in belief in the divinity of Christ played a crucial role in the fate and fortune of science, and that only such a belief shall provide moral strength for a proper use of the tools of science that have an increasingly frightening range.

In *The Savior of Science* I also dealt with evolution. In doing so I recalled that passage about water spiders, quoted above to illustrate a crucial point in coping with Darwinism, that strange mixture of incomplete science and complete philosophical obfuscation. The passage about water spiders must not be used as a proof that God created them specially and millions of other species, all of which display "skills" that Darwinism never explained scientifically. By that scientific explanation I mean the step-by-step demonstration that countless modifications of an organ did indeed lead to an organ very different and used for very different purposes. The great strength of Darwin lies in his bringing together powerful indications that allow only one inference: all species have arisen in strict dependence on the alteration of other species. Christians, who believe in an Almighty God, must be grateful to Darwin for having, however unwittingly, reminded them, that it is not the materialists who must have the strongest confidence in the unlimited power of matter about everything material, but the ones who believe in the Almighty Creator of all matter.

Darwinists can only be pitied for their often unabashed materialism. On its basis one cannot even infer that generalizations, which are their daily food, such as species, genera, phyla, kingdom, etc., are really valid ones. Even more to be pitied are those (and most Darwinists are such) who devote their entire life to the purpose of proving that there is no purpose. To prove purpose, which in man goes together with free will, let alone the analogical realization of purposeful action in animals and plants, one needs an epistemology, which, among other things, is incompatible with easy recourses to the Bible, but, as I argued in *Bible and Science,* still shines through every page of it.

So much in the way of background for the remark that in *The Savior of Science* follows another instance of water spiders:

> There is a Queensland spider called *the magnificent,* because of the fine colouring of the female. But it is her way of catching moths that concerns us at present. She hangs down from a line and spins a thread about an inch and a half in length, bearing at the free end a globule of

very viscid matter, a little larger than the head of a pin. The thread is held out by one of the front legs, and on the approach of a moth the spider whirls the thread and the globule with surprising speed. The moth is attracted, caught, pulled up, killed, and sucked. When it is touched by the whirling globule it is helpless as a fly on fly-paper. We may well say of the magnificent spider, *c'est magnifique.*

Here I remarked that the continuation of this *"c'est magnifique"* should not be *mais ce n'est pas la guerre,* whatever the endless skirmishes provoked by the illogicalities of Darwinism, but, rather, *ce n'est pas la sélection naturelle.* This is not to suggest that natural selection does not play a very important role. But in saying this one heavily relies precisely on the kind of philosophy that most champions of evolution claim to have eliminated by their science. They carefully sweep under the rug the fact that nobody has yet demonstrated *scientifically* that natural selection does indeed produce the magnificent behavior of water spiders and countless other creatures. Those who claim that such a demonstration is on hand are as mistaken as those who overlook the fact that evolutionary biology has to rely heavily on generalizations and extrapolations. And so does religion. Whenever a Christian apologist grows unmindful of this, he pulls the very ground from under his very feet. There are theological counterparts of those who no less than the purposive debunkers of purpose illustrate the darkening of the intellect, one of the chief effects of man's erstwhile Fall.

Since I began with Duhem, I perhaps should close with remarks about other works of mine connected with him. Providence (misnamed nowadays as Chance, writ large) brought me into contact around 1985 with Norbert Dufourcq of Paris. He was a prominent musicologist, the son of the famed church historian, Albert Dufourcq, who in turn was one of Duhem's best friends at the University of Bordeaux. Norbert Dufourcq thus inherited much of Duhem's correspondence as well as the correspondence of Hélène, Duhem's daughter. This connection was the source of the material that appeared in a book, *Reluctant Heroine: The Life and Work of Hélène Duhem.*[15] Her story, a very gripping one, should be of interest not only to the professional historian of science, but also to anyone wishing to know the extent to which prominent publishing firms are willing to ignore their contractual obligations and serve thereby powerful ideological interest groups in academe who just simply cannot contemplate the airing of some facts.

It was also through Providence that I met Mlle Marie-Madeleine Gallet, Albert Dufourcq's niece, who was Hélène Duhem's great support in her closing years. It was from Mlle Gallet that I obtained for publication Duhem's albums of landscape sketches. A vast selection of them appeared, with my introduction, as *The Physicist as Artist: The Landscapes of Pierre Duhem*.[16] The Académie des Sciences in Paris let me use its collection of the almost daily letters that Pierre Duhem wrote to his daughter between 1909 and 1916. A selection from them appeared, with my notes and introduction, as *Lettres de Pierre Duhem à sa fille Hélène*. All this material greatly helped me in writing *Scientist and Catholic: Pierre Duhem* that came out in French and in Spanish as well.

The full list of my publications until 1990 is available in *Creation and Scientific Creativity: A Study in the Thought of S. L. Jaki* by Paul Haffner, originally a doctoral dissertation that earned its author *summa cum laude* at the Gregorian University at Rome.[17] There one can read my statement upon my being inducted, in 1991, into the Pontifical Academy of Sciences as one of its honorary members. On that occasion I paid my homage to Duhem's memory and also voiced my view that what God had put into separate conceptual compartments, no one should try to fuse together.

I hope and pray that God will give me the strength to write a summary of my views on science and religion, the thrust of which may easily be gathered from this brief essay. Another plan of mine is now under way, under the title, *Means to Message: A Treatise on Truth*, in which I set forth my philosophy, that is, epistemology and metaphysics with an eye on science. There I will make much of what I have learned from Etienne Gilson about methodical realism, and from the Liverpool philosopher, J. E. Turner, about the logical fallacy of claims that the uncertainty relation disproved causality. There I will develop further the unique status of the category of quantities among all categories, by which I understand the ten Aristotelian categories and not their Kantian counterfeits. A foretaste of this can be found in my latest publication, a long essay entitled, "The Limits of a Limitless Science," which first appeared in Italian translation in *Con-Tratto,* as commissioned for its 1996 Yearbook, but will soon appear in English as well in the *Asbury Theological Journal* (Spring 1998).

While all talk about religion (theology) stands or falls with the philosophy it rests upon, this is less true of science. The more exact is a science, such as physics, the more its conclusions become independent of the philosophical matrix out of which they have grown. Insofar as those conclusions are quantitative, they have a validity independent of the philosophy the individual scientist tags on them. Thus science can be compared to the building of an edifice: The completed theory is like an edifice from which all the scaffolding (including philosophy) has been removed. The edifice, however, contains nothing philosophical. It is a mere structure in numbers. It is in this sense that one should take Hertz's famous dictum: "Maxwell's theory [of electromagnetism] is Maxwell's system of equations," a dictum that I cannot repeat often enough. Nothing remotely as fundamental has ever been said by a great physicist about the physical theory of an even greater physicist.

When cut to bare bones, exact science is nothing more, nothing less than a system of equations. There would be no conflict whatever between science and theology were scientists truly mindful of this truth. But scientists are, like all of us, philosophers as well. The only way to avoid philosophy is to say nothing. The trouble is that nothing can sell a bad philosophy more effectively than attaching it to a splendid science. (Thus science is turned into one of the three S's of modern life: Sports, Sex, Science, all writ large.) The converse is not true; no amount of science, insofar as it is science and not something more, can justify a single philosophical proposition and much less a single theological statement, which has to be a proposition not about how the heavens go, but how to go to Heaven. Unfortunately, theologians, believing themselves to be in possession of eternal truths, are prone to discourse about mere temporalities, such as the physical universe, about whose measures, large and small, science is the sole arbiter.

In sum, ever since science obtained its only viable birth, it keeps unfolding the enormous potentialities of its basic equations of motion. Thus science reveals more and more about the quantitative aspects of all things in relative motion to one another. In performing this revelatory function, science makes empirically, that is, measurably verifiable predictions. To perform this function science, once truly born, needs no extraneous revelation. This is why science is neither theistic, nor atheistic; it is just science, unlike theology, which has to be theistic. Theology, unless it wants to degenerate into a branch of mere religious studies, must be, at the very minimum, about a personal God, who can and must be worshiped, and not merely admired as a superior form of sunrise or sunset, or a mere mist hovering over a well-manicured lawn.

Sundays are not for communing with Nature, writ large, but for the worship of a personal God, who has absolute sovereignty even over that mankind that makes the greater mess of itself the more it lives up to its declaration of total autonomy. Modern man, so proud of his science, still has to learn that science reveals precisely the fact that the universe is restricted to do, relatively speaking, very few things. A little reflection on this may prompt any clear-thinking individual to draw the conclusion and genuflect. For the answer to the question of why is the universe such, and not something else, leads one to the ultimate cause of any suchness, or the source of all, which is Almighty God. He could have created an infinite variety of worlds. The one in existence is the result of His sovereign creative choice. This is why the actually existing universe has a stunning set of specificities whose investigation is our great intellectual stepping stone to the recognition of the One who is existence himself. For as He revealed himself, He is the One who IS.

References

1. Heinrich Hertz, *Electric Waves,* trans. D. E. Jones (New York: Dover, 1962), 21; originally published in 1893.
2. Arthur Stanley Eddington, *Science and the Unseen World* (New York: The Macmillan Company, 1930), 58.
3. J. Arthur Thomson, *Biology for Everyman* (New York: E. P. Dutton, 1935), 360.
4. Stanley L. Jaki, *Is there a Universe?* (Liverpool: Liverpool University Press, 1993).

5. Stanley L. Jaki, *God and the Cosmologists* (Edinburgh: Scottish Academic Press, 1989; new, revised, and enlarged edition, 1998).

6. Stanley L. Jaki, *The Road of Science and the Ways to God* (Chicago: University of Chicago Press, 1978).

7. Stanley L. Jaki, "Words: Blocks, Amoebas, or Patches of Fog? Artificial Intelligence and the Foundations of Fuzzy Logic," *Proceedings of the International Society for Optical Engineering* 2761 (1996), 138–143.

8. Pierre Duhem, *The Aim and Structure of Physical Theory* (Princeton: Princeton University Press, 1954), 273–74.

9. Stanley L. Jaki, *Uneasy Genius: The Life and Work of Pierre Duhem* (Dordrecht: Nijhoff, 1984).

10. Currently out of print; to be republished by Real View Books in late 1998.

11. Stanley L. Jaki, *Science and Creation: From Eternal Cycles to an Oscillating Universe* (Edinburgh: Scottish Academic Press, 1987).

12. Stanley L. Jaki, *Asbury Journal of Theology* 50 (Spring 1995), 37–49.

13. Stanley L. Jaki, *Bible and Science* (Front Royal, Va.: Christendom Press, 1996).

14. Stanley L. Jaki, "Determinism and Reality," in *Great Ideas Today 1990* (Chicago: Encyclopedia Britannica, 1990), 277–301.

15. Stanley L. Jaki, *Reluctant Heroine: The Life and Work of Hélène Duhem* (Edinburgh: Scottish Academic Press, 1991).

16. Stanley L. Jaki, *The Physicist as Artist: The Landscapes of Pierre Duhem* (Edinburgh: Scottish Academic Press, 1990).

17. Paul Haffner, *Creation and Scientific Creativity: A Study in the Thought of Stanley L. Jaki* (Front Royal, Va.: Christendom Press, 1991).

7

THE CHRISTIAN WAY

ARTHUR PEACOCKE

Any scientist, especially if connected with biology, who professes any attachment to the Christian faith is liable to encounter incredulity on the part of many acquaintances whose received mythology is that of the "warfare of science and religion." Although this mythology is well entrenched in the media, the fact is that, in recent decades and in spite of this cultural pressure, many of those engaged in the scientific enterprise have been able with intellectual integrity to follow the Christian "Way" (as it was called in the early days of the church).

Among these I include myself. The path is not always smooth from skepticism and agnosticism to faith, for continuously new challenges arise from the changing perspectives on the world from the ever-expanding horizons of scientific inquiry. This is as it should be, for any synthesis of perceptions of God, humanity, and nature must integrate, or at least be consonant with, the knowledge of humanity and nature that the sciences provide—as well as with new theological insights. So any scientist who espouses the Christian faith in any of its variegated forms must be perennially engaged in a continuous dialogue between his or her science and faith. Some are, some aren't!

I was young enough at the outbreak of war in 1939, and still young enough in 1942, not to be called up into the armed forces. So, from a semi-suburban, semi-industrial, semi-rural town, some twenty miles northwest of London, then still on the edge of fine open English countryside, I went "up" to Oxford with a scholarship in natural science to "read" chemistry. My interest in the subject had been roused mainly through some first-class teaching I had received at my local grammar school (in Watford, Hertfordshire) where I had a non-fee-paying scholarship place. My home was not at all bookish—my parents had left school at the ages of eleven and fourteen—but it was encouraging and enabling and the school provided as good an education as could have been found anywhere. The bombs were by that time falling, but the education persisted—disciplined and culturally broad—at the hands of men, and a few women, with first-class degrees from the best universities. I count myself lucky to have inherited a social system that was already providing such opportunities for those who did not come from academic, professional, or wealthy backgrounds.

By means of an Open Scholarship, I went to wartime Oxford, to a society light years away from my domestic milieu and one that was already, under the impact of the war, very different from what it had been in the 1930s (Evelyn Waugh and all that!). The Oxford chemistry school at that time had been for two decades pre-eminent in the country and outstanding in the world, vying with Harvard and Berkeley. The physical chemistry laboratory alone had five or six Fellows of the Royal Society among its ordinary lecturers and there were almost as many in the other chemistry laboratories. It was there I early learned an essential lesson of academic life—that many members of the staffs of British university departments can be as intellectually distinguished as its professorial head.

Physical chemistry appealed to me, and still does, because of its intellectual coherence and beauty—in particular kinetics, thermodynamics, and quantum theory. In fact, when I look back over my rather varied teaching career, I find I never actually stopped teaching or writing about thermodynamics in some context or other. For example, my last scientific book on the physical chemistry of biological organization was concerned with the irreversible thermodynamics of biological processes. The research I did for my first degree and subsequently for a doctorate was in the Oxford Physical Chemistry Laboratory where I worked with Sir Cyril Hinshelwood. He was himself a polymath—one of those wide-ranging products of the Oxford chemistry school—who by then had received a Nobel Prize for his work on chemical kinetics. When I joined his team, he had begun to apply his knowledge of chemical kinetics (the study of rates of chemical reactions) to the study of the processes of living organisms. I worked on the rate processes involved in the growth of bacteria and their inhibition by certain substances. I duly obtained the degree of D.Phil. and took up a post in the University of Birmingham.

In the eleven years at Birmingham, where I moved from being assistant lecturer to senior lecturer, I worked on something that had begun to interest me, namely the physical chemistry of DNA molecules. DNA at that time was only just becoming to be seen as a very big molecule—we now know, of course, that it has tens of thousands of units strung along two intertwined helical chains. There was some challenging physical chemistry to be done in relation to this extraordinary structure and I was able to engage in this with the simplest of equipment (e.g., a pH meter) but with a maximum of intellectual challenge. In 1952, I was in Berkeley on a Rockefeller Fellowship, at the distinguished Virus Laboratory headed by W. M. Stanley of tobacco mosaic virus fame, when James Watson and Francis Crick announced the structure of DNA in the British journal *Nature*. Doing primarily physicochemical work on DNA with results of interest to others in the field (we were able to ascertain that the chains in DNA were not branched and that the hydrogen bonding proposed by Watson and Crick was the only kind present in the structure), I came to be, at that time, in close contact with those working on X-ray diffraction studies and the structure of DNA.

My scientific career flourished. I went back to Oxford to a fellowship at St. Peter's College and a lectureship in the university, and there I continued to teach physical chemistry and do research in physical biochemistry. I pursued research into wider aspects of the physical chemistry of biological macromolecules. After twenty-four years of such work I had written some 120 papers and was running a research group with ten or twelve post-graduates and post-doctoral students. Then at the age of forty-eight the Oxford scientist became a Cambridge dean, the name given to the person in charge of a Cambridge college chapel, Clare College, in my case.

How did this happen and why? In some ways, Cambridge was, I suppose, the last place I expected to find myself in! So now I must tell the other story, running along alone all the time, parallel and intertwined with the one I have just told—just like the two complementary chains of DNA.

I was brought up in a typical Church of England household—typical in the sense that the established Church of England was the church my family stayed away from, except for baptisms, weddings, and funerals. I was sent to Sunday School at a local church whose "high" style of worship was disapproved of by my family (presumably it was thought to be too florid and un-English in its excesses) and later I went voluntarily to a somewhat "lower" evangelical church, in which I was confirmed. Adolescent schoolboy evangelical fervor soon gave way at Oxford to a mild undergraduate agnosticism, which I shared with most of my contemporaries. Yet we all went to college chapel (indeed scholars of my college, Exeter, *had* to do so being "on the Foundation," as it was said). At that time, in the early 1940s, it was also the accepted convention that everybody went to chapel on a Sunday evening, then to dinner in Hall, partaking of a glass of beer and then later listened to music or poetry readings in the same Hall. I was at the college of Neville Coghill, famous later for his translations and productions of Chaucer's *Canterbury Tales,* and that had a lot to do with the cultural quality of our wartime college life (perhaps I should add that Richard Burton was a contemporary, a pupil of Coghill).

Religious and philosophical questions continuously crossed my mind. I rejected biblical literalism as naive and the penal/substitutionary theory of atonement as unintelligible and immoral, an opinion I hold to this day. The urging of such views by evangelical "born-again" Christians in my undergraduate days was the chief cause of my alienation from all things Christian and of the end, for the time being, of my attachment to that faith. It took me some time to find out that other ways of thinking were possible for Christian believers. One of the turning points was hearing a sermon in the University Church by William Temple, by then Archbishop of Canterbury, and the most considerable philosopher-theologian to hold that office since Anselm. I came away aware, as I had never been before, that a *reasonable* case could be made out for Christian belief and that, although I still did not embrace it, it was an intellectually defensible and respectable position. So, the closed door became ajar. As a graduate student doing scientific research in Oxford, questions kept pressing on me—sharpened by the transparent and undogmatic faith of my wife-to-be. How *could* one explain and account for what every scientific advance unveiled and reinforced, namely the inherent intelligibility and rationality of the natural world? Both the *fact* of its existence (the answer to the question one asks, "Why is there anything at all?") and the manifest rationality of the natural world seemed to demand some kind of theistic affirmation to make any coherent sense of it all—and making sense of a wide range of data was just what my training and research experience were making my habitual intellectual practice. So the God-idea, you might say, pursued me, and my experience echoed that of the famous first lines of Francis Thompson's *The Hound of Heaven:*

> I fled Him, down the nights and down the days;
> I fled Him, down the arches of the years:
> I fled Him, down the labyrinthine ways
> Of my own mind.

The data, which we need to put together into some sort of intelligible and meaningful pattern, include human beings with all their sublime achievements and also their manifest degradations. By this time—it was now the late 1940s—my generation had seen, if only by film and photograph, what the Allied Forces had opened up in Dachau, Auschwitz, and Belsen and we had looked down into the bottomless pit of the potentiality of human evil, which the twentieth century has seen escalate with an enhanced power perhaps more than in any other.

I tried, in my own ill-informed way, to come to grips with the problem of evil—a full intellectual solution may always elude me though I am now able to narrow down and specify the problem better. It certainly became clearer then, and this still seems to me to be valid, that, even if the existence of evil raises baffling intellectual questions, and it certainly does, we have been shown how evil is to be *overcome* in reality and not just in theory. I began dimly to perceive what is sublimely expressed in the concluding stanza of Dante's *Paradiso*—where he describes his final vision of God:

> High phantasy lost power and here broke off;
> Yet, as a wheel moves smoothly, free from jars,
> My will and my desire were turned by love,
> The love that moves the sun and the other stars.

It is *love* that overcomes evil and the one Creator God, whose existence as Supreme Rationality I had begun to be driven to recognize, was also, it became clearer to me, the One whose inner character is least misleadingly described as "Love" and whose outgoing activity is an expression of that same nature that shines through the life, death, and resurrection of Jesus the Christ. So, my quest proceeded. Looking back at my time as a graduate student in physical chemistry I am just amazed how arrogantly I assumed I could learn little from the theologically informed minds all within half a mile of me and plowed my own furrow, reading my own books without asking any of the learned people around me what they thought about these matters. Perhaps one has to make one's own way, however meandering. It will always be one's own and maybe there are no short cuts.

I undertook more systematic study and, on the advice of Geoffrey Lampe, then professor of theology at Birmingham University, I even managed to get a degree in theology. I was deeply influenced (and still am) by the writings of judiciously reasonable theologians—William Temple, Charles Raven, Ian Ramsey, and Lampe himself. I could not then, and do not now— and here my formation (my *Bildung*) as a scientist comes out—accept any automatic authority of church or scripture *per se*. For me, belief must meet the general criteria of reasonableness, or inference to the best explanation. This is still my position, although it is coupled with a growing awareness of our dependence on the earliest witnesses to Jesus as the Christ and of our need to sit at the feet of the men and women of God of all ages, traditions, and religions.

I was relieved to discover that the much press-besieged and battered Church of England (our part of the Anglican Communion) was theologically, philosophically, and intellectually a very *broad* church, providing the space in which to move and grow, feeding as it does, on both Catholic and Reformed traditions and influenced too by the Eastern Orthodox (and indeed the ancient Celtic) churches. It has long had the habit of emphasizing the role, in the formation of a securely based and stable faith, of the use of reason based on experience in sifting both Scripture and Tradition. Its reliance on this "three-legged stool" of Scripture-Tradition-Reason could in fact claim to be its own special distinctive feature, since other churches tend to rely more exclusively on Scripture or Tradition.

It is instructive, in this connection, and in view of my own personal synthesis of science and religion, to read what the first historian of the Royal Society wrote in 1667 about the relation of church and science, the new natural philosophy. Remember, the Royal Society had only been founded a few years before, almost concurrently with the restoration of the *Book of Common Prayer* and of the Church of England after the Commonwealth had abolished them.

This historian, Thomas Sprat, wrote:

> . . . We behold the agreement that is between the present *Design* of the *Royal Society* and that of our Church [of England] in its beginning. They both may lay equal claim to the word *Reformation;* the one having compassed it in *Religion,* the other purposing it in *Philosophy.* They both have taken a like course to bring this about; each of them referring themselves to the perfect *Originals* for their instruction; the one to the Scripture, the other to the large Volume of the *Creatures.* . . . They both suppose alike, that their *Ancestors* might err; and yet retain a sufficient reverence for them. . . . The *Church of England* therefore may justly be styl'd *Mother* of this sort of *Knowledge;* and so the care of its *nourishment* and prosperity peculiarly lyes upon it.

Supposing "our ancestors might err" and yet retaining a "sufficient reverence for them" seems to me just the right balance between destructive radicalism, on the one hand, and dogmatic traditionalism, on the other. So I count myself fortunate that, at that stage of my quest, I had the chance of pursuing it within the ranks of a Christian church that is the reformed and the catholic church of my own people—one that had, and still has, the habit of allowing open inquiry into the reasonableness of faith in the light of modern (in my case scientific) knowledge.

Theological study showed me something I had *not* expected, such is the myopia of the professional scientist, namely that the Christian church throughout the ages has, behind its shifting and variable facade, a very tough-minded intellectual tradition of its own, which makes the content of its thought a worthy and proper subject of university study—the message I had begun to pick up in that sermon of William Temple. Figures such as Paul, Origen, Gregory of Nyssa, Augustine, Anselm, Aquinas, among many others, are intellectual giants and simply cannot be ignored by any twentieth-century seeker after intelligibility and meaning.

Naturally, I always found myself relating my scientific world view to theological perspectives. I found I could not ignore the continuity and interchange in the human being between physical, mental, aesthetic, and spiritual activities and the knowledge we gain from them. In theology, this meant I would place, and still do, a strong emphasis on the *sacramental,* which is, in the realm of theology, the concept that unites the physical, the mental, the aesthetic, and the spiritual. I had for some ten years or so been what the Church of England calls a "lay reader" and so had been authorized to conduct non-sacramental public worship and to preach. But this increasingly felt like trying to walk on one leg, especially as the synthesis of the scientific and Christian aspects of my life and thinking was occurring increasingly through the sacraments and the sacramental aspects of all life. This meant I experienced a growing urge to celebrate sacramentally our unitary awareness of nature, humanity, and God.

Some years before, I had begun to think of ordination to the priesthood as a "worker-priest," that is, in my case, a "priest-scientist." In the event, after an abortive attempt at a change of career, and some twelve years after my beginning to think of it, I was ordained in 1971 first to the diaconate and then to the priesthood in Christ Church Cathedral, Oxford.

I shared, and still share, all the average Englishman's conditioned reflexes toward and suspicions of the clergy as a class, so I was glad to become a priest but had no intention then, and still do not have (I hope I have avoided it), of becoming a "clergyman." After ordination, I intended to continue as a priest-scientist, a university research worker and teacher in priest's orders doing my job with and alongside everyone else. Such I have always regarded myself.

During my years in Cambridge, I found something about myself of which I had not previously been totally aware, namely, that the scientific "me" could not be totally absorbed without remainder into the priest, even one working on the relation of science and faith. Thus it was that, because I was free from faculty pressure to publish conventional papers (this time scientific ones), I was able to explore widely, in a way I was never able to do while heading a scientific research group, into new developments, some still speculative, in physicochemical theory that were beginning to look exceedingly promising. These developments pertained to the interpretation of the hitherto baffling complexity of living organisms and their intricate processes. This eventually—although it was a long haul, taking ten years—resulted in the publication of my scientific monograph on the physical chemistry of biological organization. I brought together many previously unconnected developments in mathematics, kinetics, and thermodynamics and I hope made a contribution to our understanding of the wonder of biological complexity in the natural world.

No one engaged in working on the interface between science and religion can be unaware of the social dimension of this interaction: the communities of those engaged in the scientific and theological enterprises are estranged and alienated and each goes its own way regardless of the other. Over the years I have been able to play some part in breaking this silence, of crossing this "no man's land" between two groups cast by many in the role of opposing armies by inherited, and false, mythologies of what happened in the nineteenth, and earlier, centuries. In the early 1970s, I started in Britain informal consultations between scientists, theologians, and clergy who were concerned to relate their scientific knowledge and methods of study to their religious faith and practice. This initially small group grew in numbers as it faced these increasingly complex issues and in 1975 the Science and Religion Forum was formally inaugurated at Durham. It has been meeting annually and publishing its deliberations and reviews of relevant books ever since. Parallel, though mostly smaller, groups concerned with these themes were all this time coming into existence in other parts of Europe. After an initial exploratory consultation convened by me in September 1984, at Clare College, Cambridge, the first European conference on Science and Religion was held, with Dr. Karl Schmitz-Moomann (the other initiator of the project) in the chair, at the Evangelische Akademie at Loccum in the Federal Republic of Germany on the topic of "Evolution and Creation" (*not*, be it noted, on "creationism," which appeared in our deliberations only through its rejection). There followed a second European conference in 1988, and at the third in Geneva in 1990 the European Society for the Study of Science and Theology was formally inaugurated. All of this is immensely encouraging and of great significance for the future of religion, in general, and of Christianity, in particular, in western society.

Much of the preceding account has referred to the concerns of the "head," but the "heart" too has its reasons. Indeed, for more than thirty years I had been intuiting, instinctively discerning, that a purely intellectual dialogue between those engaged in the scientific and theological enterprises was not enough. For theology, "theo-logy," is *ex hypothesi* concerned with words about God—and words restrict and confine. God is in "the still small voice" and in the silences that follow louder, more articulate exercises. "Theo-logy," cannot itself be the experience of God who is known through life in prayer, in worship, and in silence. I saw that the church needs not only intellectual inquiry of the kind stimulated by the bodies I described, but it needs a cadre of committed and informed members to constitute a new kind of "Dominican" order, held together by prayer and sacrament, and committed to the life of science for and on behalf of the church: to represent the church in science and science in the church.

So it was that in 1987 there was founded, initially within the Church of England, a new dispersed Order. The Society of Ordained Scientists (S.O.Sc.), is held together by a Rule of prayer and sacrament, to which we are committed through appropriate vows made at an annual Eucharist presided over in its first nine years by the then Archbishop of York, Dr. John Habgood, who was himself formerly a research physiologist. The constitution has been so framed that the Society now includes among its members not only priests of the Anglican Communion, including six women priest-scientists, but also ministers of other churches; it also has a North American chapter. I see its future as wide open and as having great potential significance for the church in its relation to science, technology, and medicine (we have already been able to be a useful resource for it in a number of ways); and as having expanded ecumenical possibilities, for example, with the relatively recently formed body, "Jesuits in Science."

I conclude with some general reflections prompted by this retrospect on my life, which has somehow always been spent on borderlines, whether of physics/chemistry, physical chemistry/biochemistry, or science/theology. First of all, *Christian belief,* or indeed any religious belief, it seems to me, will confine itself to an intellectual and cultural ghetto unless it relates its affirmations to the best knowledge we have of the world around us (and that includes the human world). This is a perennial challenge to Christian theology and to all religious belief, one that, at certain times in the past, Christian thinkers have responded to superbly and creatively. The problem today is that few theologians, and indeed few students of the humanities, have any inkling of the breadth and depth of the scientific world view—partly because of the extraordinary narrowness of most education systems, notably that in the United Kingdom. There is an immense work of general education needed everywhere before religious belief can begin to engage creatively with the new perceptions on the world that science now affords. Myriads of particular questions still arise, such as:

- the nature and destiny of humanity in the light of its evolutionary origins;
- human needs and potentialities and the nature of the human person in the light of new knowledge from human psychology, the cognitive sciences, genetics—to name a few;
- our attitudes to nature and our influence on it;

- how to talk about God's action in the light of the increasing likelihood that the universe seems to have inbuilt *self*-creative potentialities;
- human beings appear to be "rising beasts" rather than "fallen angels."

And so one could go on. Such issues, and many others, cannot be ducked and will not go away.

Secondly, the *sciences,* through their range and diversity, now provide a perspective on the world whose full emotional and poetic force really needs to be conveyed by a twentieth-century Dante. That perspective indeed sharpens the questions we ask about personal meaning and intelligibility, for example: What kind of universe is it that the original fluctuation in a quantum field—the primeval mass of baryons and quarks and neutrinos and light quanta—could over eons of time by its own inbuilt potentiality and form develop into human beings who espouse values, truth, beauty, and goodness, and could become a Newton, a Mozart, a Jesus of Nazareth?

Thirdly, the *relation of science to theology* is just one of the problems of the relations of many disciplines and forms of knowledge to each other. We need today a new map of knowledge. Science shows the natural world to be a hierarchy of levels of complexity, each operating at its own level, each requiring its own methods of study and developing its own conceptual framework, and so its own science. In light of this, I affirm that atoms and molecules are not *more* real than cells or populations of cells, or human communities, or human persons. There are *social* and *personal* facts just as there are physical and biochemical ones. In my view, the interpretation of the relation between these different levels should not be what has been called "nothing buttery," that is, reductionism. Biology is *not* nothing but physics and chemistry; neurophysiology is *not* nothing but biochemistry; psychology is *not* nothing but neurophysiology; sociology is *not* nothing but biology. All the way up the hierarchy of complexity we see these takeover bids by the level below with respect to the level above. However, each level refers to only one aspect of reality and we need explicitly to understand the nonexclusive relations they bear to each other.

Furthermore, the scientific and theological enterprise both involve *exploration* into the nature of reality. This comes as no surprise to those studying science. However, very few people these days (many of whom, especially politicians in Britain, use the word "theology" pejoratively), seem to regard the theological enterprise as also an exploration into the nature of reality. But that is indeed what it is, as splendidly expressed in the opening sentence of the 1976 report of the Doctrine Commission of the Church of England on *Christian Believing:*

> Christian life is an adventure, a voyage of discovery, a journey, sustained by faith and hope, towards a final and complete communion with the Love at the heart of all things.

Let me not pretend that in my explorations I have arrived anywhere of universal significance. There is a mystery at the heart of things, which requires not only all the data to be assembled together and none to be dismissed, but also the most intensive application of mind and heart and will to penetrate. The great Newton recognized, as a scientist, that, if he had seen further than others (he certainly had!), it was "by standing on the shoulders of giants." This is as true for religion as it is for science. Newton's also great successor, Einstein, remarked, "Science without religion is lame, religion without science is blind."

One's formation as a scientist irrevocably stamps one with the urge to ask "Why?" and "What is the evidence for?" in all matters, not least those concerning Christian belief. I have found that the disjunction experienced in relation to the frequent incredulity of those, especially scientists, when confronted with the existence of a *priest*-scientist, is matched by the incomprehension of traditionally trained clergy who have no perception whatever of the challenge of the scientific world view to received Christian belief. They just cannot understand where many of us priest-scientists are "coming from" in our theological questionings which, to them, seem tinged with unwarranted skepticism. We continue to go on asking the "Why?" questions imprinted in our approach to all phenomena, both natural and "religious."

In all of these spiritual experiences of a natural scientist, my *religio philosophy naturalis,* there is one precondition that all explorers into realities, natural and divine, must fulfill. It was the attitude expressed in a prayer of that devout man, Sir Thomas Browne:

> Teach my endeavours so thy workes to read,
> That learning them, in Thee I may proceed.

This need for humility has never been better expressed than by that arch-hammer of ecclesiastics and Darwin's "bull-dog," Thomas H. Huxley, who wrote in a letter to Charles Kingsley, the author and evangelical clergyman:

> Science seems to me to teach in the highest and strongest manner the great truth which is embodied in the Christian conception of entire surrender to the will of God. Sit down before fact as a little child, be prepared to give up every preconceived notion, follow humbly wherever and to whatever abysses Nature leads, or you shall learn nothing. I have only begun to learn content and peace of mind since I resolved at all risks to do this.

8

PHYSICIST AND PRIEST

JOHN POLKINGHORNE

The course of my spiritual pilgrimage has not been punctuated by events of high drama. There have, of course, been moments of deeper insight and greater commitment, but no striking reversals that would call for the use of a Damascus road kind of language.

My engagement with religion is older than my engagement with science. I grew up in a Christian home and, though my parents did not speak much about their religion, it was clearly central to their lives. I absorbed from them a recognition of the spiritual dimension of life and I acquired the habit of churchgoing, which has remained with me throughout my life.

I was a clever little boy, particularly good at mathematics, and it was natural that when eventually I went to university it was to study for a maths degree. During my undergraduate days at Trinity College, Cambridge, I became fascinated by the way in which the search for mathematical beauty is the key to unlocking the secrets of the physical universe. Consequently, when I came to do a Ph.D., I chose to work on a problem in quantum field theory (the basic formalism necessary to describe the behavior of elementary particles). This led to a long career as a theoretical physicist, in the course of which I became professor of mathematical physics at Cambridge and the senior member of a large and active research group.

During this time there were certain constant factors that defined and sustained my religious life. One was the figure of Jesus Christ. There is something mysterious and compelling, exciting and profoundly hopeful about him, which means that for me no view of the meaning and purpose of existence would begin to be adequate which did not take Christ fully into account. There is the strangeness of his end—deserted by his friends, enduring the darkness from which he cries, "My God, my God, why have you forsaken me?", an apparent total failure—and yet the certainty that that was not the end (for otherwise, we would surely never have heard of him), which leads me to a belief in the Resurrection.

Another enduring factor is the experience of worship. I am a pretty humdrum Christian; my life has not contained the depths of a profound mystical experience of unity or the height of an awe-inspiring encounter with the numinous otherness of God. Instead my spirituality centers on a regular life of private prayer and scripture-reading and the weekly eucharistic gathering of the Christian community in which we obey the command to "do this" in memory of Christ. In a way which I find hard to explain, but which is essential and sustaining for me, these practices are at the heart of my continuing spiritual life.

All the time I was a working scientist I felt no critical tension between my scientific and my religious beliefs. It never seemed a question of either/or, but rather a question of both/and, if one were to do justice to the richness of experience and truth. I am quite happy to accept big bang cosmology and evolutionary history and also to believe that the Creator's will and purpose are behind it all. There are, of course, puzzles about how scientific and theological insights relate to each other but I have never felt I detected a head-on collision between them.

In my middle forties two things began to happen. One was that I began to consider how I should spend the rest of my life. I had greatly enjoyed being part of the theoretical physics community, but I recognized that in mathematically based subjects one tends to make one's most useful contribution in the first half of one's working life. I occupied a responsible position and I did not want to continue in it beyond the time in which I could manage to make a reasonable contribution to the progress of work in our research group. This feeling was reinforced by the fact that my subject had just completed a significant period in its development (the discovery of the quark structure of matter) and was now beginning to move off in a totally new direction. Moreover, in my family life, our children had reached the stage where they were becoming more independent of their parents and this meant that my wife and I recovered a certain room for maneuver within our own lives. I began to think that I had done my little bit for theoretical physics and that it was time to decide what to do next.

The second thing that was happening to me was that I had joined a group that met every fortnight to study the Bible and to engage in serious discussion of theological issues. The group was led by my friend Eric Hutchison, an Anglican priest, a former lecturer in theology at Makere College in Uganda, and a Jungian psychotherapist. Eric is a brilliant teacher and expositor and participation in this group over a period of years opened my eyes to the richness and excitement of theological thinking. This experience was a powerful influence on me as I pondered what my next step in life should be.

It had to be a joint decision with my wife, Ruth, as it clearly affected her as much as me. I suppose that if there were to be a dramatic moment in my pilgrimage, this would have been the place for it, but in actual fact the decision to resign my professorship and train for the Anglican priesthood was one that formed clearly but unspectacularly, over a period of two or three months, fortunately in both our minds.

I had to have my vocation assessed by the Church authorities—an experience I found helpful and supportive—and I had to tidy up my academic affairs and make sure I did not leave my research students in the lurch. All this took about eighteen months. My colleagues in theoretical physics were naturally surprised and some were intrigued. I had a number of conversations with different friends in different laboratories in Europe and North America, in the course of which I tried to explain, in response to questioning, what I was up to and why Christian belief was so central and important for me that it made this step a sensible one to take. Later on, these conversations recurred to my mind and I began to see what ideally I should have said had I had the time and wit to develop the theme properly. This led to my first book about matters of science and religion, *The Way the World Is,* published in 1983 and still in print.[1]

Meanwhile I had to train for the ministry. October 1979, just before my forty-ninth birthday, saw me enrolled as a student at Westcott House, an Anglican seminary in Cambridge. It was odd becoming a student again in middle age (it is easier to lecture than to listen!), but I enjoyed very much the experience and the company of my talented younger fellow students. I learned many things at Westcott, from Greek and Hebrew to systematic theology and on to how to work with multiply handicapped children, but the most important lesson I derived from my time there was the spiritual value of the Daily Office. As an Anglican priest I am under the obligation to say morning and evening prayer (with their use of the Psalms and Scripture) faithfully, day by day, week by week, year by year. I have found that this provides just the disciplined framework for my life that I need. I don't say that I don't sometimes feel tired and wish I didn't have to, and just occasionally, if my routine is badly disrupted, I can even forget, but the Office remains the valued staple diet of my religious observance.

About this time, I made a new contact which has proved of great importance to me. A nun, who had attended some of my lectures when she was a Cambridge student, wrote to me and through her I came to know the Society of the Sacred Cross, an Anglican religious community following a Cistercian way of life, just over the Welsh border, outside Monmouth. Tymawr Convent has become my spiritual home. I pray regularly for the sisters, and they for me, and I try to visit there once a year, part of which time is spent in a silent retreat. Not speaking to anyone for a few days, other than to God in the regular round of services, may sound a bit odd and a bit boring, but in fact it is spiritually refreshing and recenters one's life on spiritual reality.

The English are great believers in the apprentice system, learning on the job, and it is certainly the case that there is a lot about the life of a priest that one can only learn by living it, initially under the guidance of someone more experienced. Consequently those newly ordained in the Church of England are required for three years to "serve their title," that is to say to be a curate, an assistant clergyman supervised by the vicar of the parish in which they are working. I served my title in a large working-class parish in South Bristol. I spent a lot of my time wandering round the parish, meeting people, knocking on doors, and just seeing what happened. It was all rather different from the life of a Cambridge don, but I enjoyed it very much, not least because of my wise and friendly vicar, Peter Chambers.

As my time in Bristol was coming to an end, I had a totally unexpected and traumatic experience. I became very seriously ill for the first time in my life. I found myself in the Bristol Royal Infirmary, connected to various drips as I recovered from an emergency operation. My world had suddenly been drastically reduced to the confines of a hospital bed. I was very weak, God seemed infinitely far away, and I found it difficult to the point of impossibility to pray. In all this, however, I was very conscious of being prayed for, by my family, by my church, and by the sisters at Tymawr. Twice I had a sort of waking dream, or vision I suppose one might say, of a sister kneeling in the chapel at Tymawr, motionless in silent prayer before the altar, as I had so often seen them praying on my visits there. This vision was a great source of encouragement to me and I felt I had learned something of the communion Christians can have with each other through prayer.

Recovery was slow but eventually I was restored to full health and I went off to be a vicar on my own at Blean, a largish village just outside Canterbury. As I had tramped the streets of Bristol, I had, between pastoral visits, thought on and off about the relationship between the scientific and theological views of reality. A book slowly formed in my mind but it was only when I got to Blean that I had the time to begin writing it. The result was *One World.*[2] The title encapsulates what I believe about the twin preoccupations of my life, science and religion: that they are both seeking different, yet complementary, aspects of the truth about the single, many-layered world of human experience.

After being a vicar for two years, I talked to my bishop about how things were going. I explained that I was very happy in the parish, but I hoped that in the longer term I would find an opportunity also to use the more intellectual side of me than was possible in a purely pastoral setting. A few months later, quite unsought and unexpected, I received the offer to return to Cambridge as the Dean of Trinity Hall. This would be a job part pastoral and part academic. I explained to my bishop that the job had attractions for me but that I was also troubled at the thought of leaving the parish so soon. He said to me that I appeared to have been offered the kind of position I had described to him at our earlier interview and he thought I ought to think seriously about accepting it. Eventually I did.

My decision was influenced by a conviction that had grown on me in the course of the first few years of my ordained ministry, that part of my vocation was to think and write about the interrelationship of science and theology. During the ten years that I have been back in Cambridge, this has been my major intellectual preoccupation and I have written a number of books on the subject. The books do not constitute the unrolling of a predetermined plan, for I can only see my way a book ahead at a time. A topic comes into my thoughts (natural theology; divine providential action; how one with scientific habits of thought approaches the justification of fundamental Christian belief; the differences now emerging between the approaches of my scientist-theologian colleagues, Ian Barbour and Arthur Peacocke, and myself). I spend about a year thinking and reading around it. Eventually so many thoughts are buzzing about in my mind that the only way to bring some order to them is to attempt to write down what it all amounts to. This act of crystallization is very important for me. I am one of those people who does not know what he thinks until he writes it down.

I am a very concise writer. I think this is partly a result of my scientific training: one learns to write what one wants to say and then stop, resisting any temptation to reiteration or undue elaboration. I also love the act of writing, the search for the right word or phrase. It is one of the great pleasures of my life. The result has been a series of short books of about 120 pages, though my Gifford Lectures *(Science and Christian Belief,* published in America as *The Faith of a Physicist)* are longer because they seek to tackle central questions of Christian faith in a sequence of chapters woven round quotations from the Nicene Creed.[3]

Associated with this writing activity has been a good deal of speaking around, ranging from academic lectures to addresses to clergy and other conferences and talks to small groups of interested people. The best part of such occasions is the question and comment period at the end. Then one is listening and responding to the actual concerns of people. I am greatly struck by the frequency with which the problem of evil and suffering emerges in the conversation, whatever the topic of the preceding talk may have been. There is a very great mystery here and I always want to be careful not to suggest that there is some easy answer to this painful perplexity. Nevertheless, I am glad that there is some modest help that I believe science can offer us. We have learned that we live in an evolving universe. Theologically that can be understood as God having created not a ready-made world, but something more profound than that: a world that can make itself. It is the Creator's gift of love to have given this freedom to the creation to be and to make itself. The biologists tell us that there is a necessary cost of such a fruitful history. Exactly the same biochemical processes that permit cells to mutate and bring about new forms of life—the very process that drives evolution—will inevitably enable other cells to mutate and become malignant. The presence of cancer in creation is not due to divine incompetence or oversight; it is the necessary cost of an evolving world.

I do not for a moment suggest that this scientific insight is sufficient to remove the agony and anger parents might feel at seeing their child die of leukemia. The Christian answer to the problem of suffering is much more profound than that. The Christian God is not a benevolent spectator of the agony of creation but a fellow-sufferer with it. We believe that in the cross of Christ we see God embracing and accepting the darkness of human dereliction and pain and thereby bringing about its eventual defeat. This world by itself does not make total sense, but the resurrection of Christ is the seed from which a transformed and healed new creation has begun to grow. These mysterious and moving thoughts are central to my own Christian belief and hope. They make religious belief possible for me.

After I had been at Trinity Hall for three years I received an unexpected invitation to become the president of another Cambridge College, Queens'. Once again I had to think carefully about the move, for being president is a purely secular job and I had not been ordained with a view to becoming an academic administrator. However, two things persuaded me that I should accept. One is that Cambridge colleges are small academic communities in which staff and students share a common life and so to become head of one is much more than simply playing a part in running an institution. There is a kind of pastoral dimension to it. The other consideration was that Queens', like all the historic colleges at Cambridge, is a religious as well as a learned foundation. We have a college chapel and successive deans have been kind and hospitable to me in allowing me fully to share in its worship, so that I preach and celebrate the Eucharist regularly.

I am writing this in the final year of my presidency. In retirement, God willing, I hope to continue to think and write and lecture. I also hope to find some honorary part-time way in which I can continue to exercise a priestly ministry. My life has been varied and not without its surprises, particularly over the last seventeen years. When I turned my collar round and became a clergyman, many things changed for me. Yet many things remained the same. Of these latter, two have been of the greatest significance. In both my careers, first as a scientist and then as a thinker on theological issues, I have been concerned with the search for truth, the quest for an understanding of the rich reality of human experience at all its levels. Throughout my life, whether as a physicist or as a priest and all the time as a human being, I have been sustained by the practice of prayer and the sharing in the sacrament, inspired by the figure of Christ and filled with a hope that centers on him and that extends beyond death to the life of the world to come.

References

1. John Polkinghorne, *The Way the World Is* (London: Triangle, 1983; and Grand Rapids, Mich.: Eerdmans, 1983).
2. John Polkinghorne, *One World* (London: SPCK, 1986; and Princeton: Princeton University Press, 1987).
3. John Polkinghorne, *Science and Christian Belief* (London: SPCK, 1994). This book was published in the United States under the title *The Faith of a Physicist* (Princeton: Princeton University Press/Fortress, 1994, 1996).

9

TOWARD A DISTINCTIVE

MINISTRY

RUSSELL STANNARD

How did I become a Christian? I'm not altogether sure. There was certainly no dramatic conversion moment; no abrupt turning point in my life. Religion sort of crept up on me unawares. I suppose it happened something like this:

My early years were dominated by the Second World War. I spent most of the time between the ages of eight and fourteen away from home. In common with most children living in London, my younger brother Don and I were evacuated to another part of the country to escape the bombing. We went to live with our grandmother. She was a fearsome disciplinarian, ruling the household with a rod of iron. She regularly handed out beatings and other forms of punishment—as she had earlier done when bringing up my mother and her nine other children.

She had long since refused to set foot ever again in the local Anglican village church because of a row she had had with the vicar over the slovenly way he leaned on the pulpit when delivering his sermons. She couldn't bear people "slouching about"; one had to sit up straight, or stand up straight. Although the church was off limits, she insisted we go to Sunday School—at the Methodist chapel. That's where I had my initiation into the Christian faith.

After three years my brother and I were able to take advantage of a comparative lull in the bombing to return home to London. A year later I passed an examination that allowed me to go to Archbishop Tenison's Grammar School. The school, however, was itself evacuated to the outskirts of the small town of Reading. So that is where I had to spend the next two years of the war.

During that time I lived in the beautiful home of a wealthy company director and his wife, a former fashion photographer. Having myself been brought up in a working class neighborhood, it was like stepping into a different world. Auntie Bee and Uncle Bill (as I came to call them) were God-fearing, kindly people. It was taken as a matter of course that I would accompany them each Sunday to church. I went out of a sense of duty. We became great friends, and long after the war I continued to visit them until they passed away. I still have a brass telescope Uncle Bill gave me—a memento of cold nights he and I used to spend stargazing through it.

With the ending of the war, the school transferred back to London, and at long last I was able to return home permanently. My parents had thankfully survived the bombing unhurt despite numerous close calls, and the apartment block where we lived, though severely damaged by a flying bomb that landed across the road from it, still stood.

My mother was the sort of person who went to church at Easter and Christmas. My father never went; he had no time for religion, regarding it as something women did. Released from any sense of obligation to go to church regularly, I went twice a year to keep my mother company. So, I learned little from my parents about religion.

Nevertheless, they were wonderful parents, and I can never thank them enough for all they did for me. They came from the humblest of backgrounds. My father was a doorman for a block of offices, and my mother worked as a conductress on the buses. Neither had had any education beyond the age of fourteen. In the neighborhood where we lived, education was not highly regarded. On winning the scholarship that had taken me to the grammar school, the headmaster of my elementary school had hauled me out in front of the whole school as an example to the rest. I can still hear him declaiming, "This boy is on the first rung of the ladder!" Before this, they had never in living memory had a child pass anything—it was that kind of school. And yet my parents scrimped and saved and sacrificed so that I could stay on at school beyond normal school-leaving age in order that I might gain further qualifications to get me into university. Then followed three years for my first degree, followed by a further three while I got my doctorate. My father used to tease me by asking me when I was going to become "a proper man and get a job like everyone else." But I was always aware that in his heart he sensed that "all this education" was important to me, and he took an obvious pride in the progress I was making.

I am not sure how it came about, but there had always been some link between my grammar school and the church of St. Martin's-in-the-Fields, at Trafalgar Square. It must have been that Tenison had been associated with that church before he had become archbishop. Whatever the reason, it was the tradition that the school held an annual service at the church. Being the head boy for my last two years at the school, I had the responsibility at these services to mount the pulpit to read one of the lessons. There was something about these occasions—about the whole atmosphere of St. Martin's—that immediately struck a chord with me. I can only call it the "sense of the numinous." It was a very special feeling, and I felt drawn to the place. I wanted to go again.

Then came the day (I must have been seventeen or eighteen at the time) when I felt compelled to tell my father that I wanted to go to church. I don't know why, but that was one of the most difficult conversations I have ever had. He simply could not understand why anyone (particularly a *man*) would want to do such a thing. But that is how I began attending St. Martin's.

Soon after, my Aunt Letty suggested to my brother that he ought to get confirmed. She was his godmother, and took her responsibilities seriously. As my godparents had died, she also took it upon herself to suggest that I, being Don's elder brother, ought to be setting him a good example by becoming confirmed myself. So we enrolled in confirmation classes at St. Martin's Church. They were conducted by the Rev. Austin Williams, who at that time was a curate there. The classes were completely informal; we worked through no set syllabus—at least none that I could discern. Our meetings consisted of chats about

Christianity. I don't now remember what I specifically learned from Williams by way of doctrine during those classes, but I do know I was profoundly affected. It was the first time I had felt that I was truly in the presence of a man of God. If I had had any doubts about whether I was a Christian at the start of those classes, I had none at the end. It was very much a case of religion being caught rather than taught. I said earlier that I had had no dramatic conversion experience, and that is true. But if I were forced to choose a period of transition, it would have to be those classes.

Mind you, in the years to come I was unsure as to whether my faith would last. I used to sit there in church on Sunday and worry about what the future held. Would this faith that had crept up on me and taken possession of me, continue to hold me, or would it just as mysteriously slip away? As I agonized anxiously over this, it was very much a case of "Lord, I believe; help Thou my unbelief." It was to be a very long time, indeed a matter of decades, before these concerns subsided and I was left with the realization that my relationship with God had become so real, so much part of me, that it was now inconceivable that it could be otherwise. I sometimes wish I had a time machine, one that would allow me to go back in time and reassure that doubt-ridden but earnest young man that used to be me that he was indeed to remain true to the faith.

A major part of that growing confidence I owe to someone I met in my early thirties. By then I was married and had started a family, and was attending the church of St. Andrew in Roxbourne. It was an ordinary modern church in an ordinary suburb of North London, but there was nothing ordinary about the vicar, the Rev. Edward Nadkarni. He was from India. As a boy he had been appalled by the heartless way his mother had been rejected by family and "friends" on the death of his father. According to custom, she and her children no longer had any status in society. The only love and compassion to be shown to them at this traumatic time came from Christian missionaries. The young Edward converted to Christianity. On emigrating to England, he became an ordained minister in the Anglican Church. Nad, as he was affectionately known by one and all, retained throughout his life the zeal of the convert. His passionate, single-minded devotion to the

Lord Jesus put us all to shame. He was totally intolerant of anything that smacked of lukewarm, half-hearted religion. This, on a number of occasions, led to stormy scenes. (He was quick of temper, but equally quick to ask forgiveness.) These fiery eruptions led to the loss of several members of the congregation—those who found his calls for total commitment too uncomfortable to bear. But he instilled in others the deepest devotion. For us he was an inspiration, a man utterly dedicated to God. He earned from me a respect and an affection such as I had never experienced before or since. Twenty years after his untimely death of a heart attack in his mid-fifties, I still have a photograph of him over the desk in my study at home.

It was Nad who suggested to me that I ought to train to become a reader. A reader in the Church of England is a form of lay preacher. At that time I had never heard of them, but on learning about their work, I realized that Nad was right; it was exactly the kind of way I could contribute more effectively to the work of the church. Three years later I had completed my training and ascended the pulpit once more, no longer as a nervous school boy reading a lesson, but as someone embarking on a preaching ministry.

Readers are unpaid church workers. They have a distinctive ministry in that they come from all walks of life and have the widest possible variety of full-time jobs. It is the fact that they spend their working day in the secular world that can lend to their preaching a special quality of relevance—a common touch that is sometimes lacking in clergy who have gone straight from school to seminary, and from there into the ordained ministry.

It soon became clear what form my own distinctive ministry should take. By then I was a scientist, a physics lecturer at University College London after a year spent at the Radiation Laboratory at Berkeley, California. I was now engaged in research into high energy nuclear physics at the Rutherford Laboratory, Harwell, and at CERN, the European center for nuclear physics research at Geneva, Switzerland. People found it odd that a scientist should also be a preacher. Weren't science and religion incompatible? they would ask. I began to be invited to give talks and to lead discussions on the subject—mostly in schools for the benefit of sixteen- to eighteen-year-olds. In the process, I had to clarify my own thoughts on how I saw my science relating to my religion. I noticed time and again that when I gave one of these talks I would be asked whether there was a book on the subject that the young people could read if they wished to delve more deeply. At that time there was really nothing I could recommend.

Matters came to a head when I received an invitation to go to the Channel Islands and conduct a whole day of talks and discussions about science and religion for 150 school children drawn from all over Jersey. Their enthusiasm was so great that, in the absence of there being a book, a significant proportion of them bought audiotapes of the whole day's proceedings. On returning home, I promptly set to and wrote my first book, *Science and the Renewal of Belief* (SCM Press, 1982).

That opened the floodgates. The invitations to speak and to debate the issues now came from far and wide. I began appearing on TV and radio. This was partly because by then I had left University College London and had joined the newly created Open University. This was the first university of its kind, teaching mature students through specially written texts, and through programs broadcast on the main BBC TV and radio channels. Twenty-seven years after its birth, the OU has grown to become by far and away the United Kingdom's largest university with 140,000 students. In working for the OU I gained in expertise at broadcasting as well as writing. Thus it was I began reaching wider audiences in regard to discussions on science and religion.

Throughout this period I was very much aware of the difficulties encountered whenever anyone tries to bridge the gap between subject areas. By training, background, and natural inclination, one invariably approaches the divide from one of the two sides. There is always the danger of making a fool of oneself when venturing to speak outside the safe domain of one's own specialism. Despite my earlier theological training as a reader, my expertise clearly lay on the side of science, and there were times when I felt uncomfortably exposed when it came to theology. In an effort partly to redress this balance, I took a year off from physics (1987–88) and spent it at the Center of Theological Inquiry at Princeton, New Jersey. It was a fascinating experience to find myself in day-to-day company with theologians and philosophers of religion. I felt that only with such immersion could I sensitize myself to some of the concerns felt on that other side of the divide. My stay at CTI led to the book *Grounds for Reasonable Belief* (Scottish Academic Press, 1989).

Around this time, through the encouragement of my wife, Maggi, who was a school teacher, I became interested in writing for young children: mainly ten- to twelve-year-olds. I wanted to convey to them some of the excitement I had myself experienced when being introduced to modern physics, especially Einstein's Theory of Relativity. I had long since recognized how difficult it was to interest adults in the subject. "Oh, I was never any good at physics," or "But surely you have to be a genius to understand any of that" were typical reactions. When I had persisted in explaining to them how nothing could travel faster than light, and how, as you go fast, time slows down and space squashes up, they would look at me with incredulity and exclaim that it simply could not be so; it went against common sense. Then I came across a saying of Einstein himself in which he declared that common sense consists of those layers of prejudice laid down in the mind prior to the age of eighteen. It was that statement that led me to the conclusion that one had to get in quick with relativity before the mind became too accustomed to the idea that there was only the one time and the one space; I had to strike before the mind became fossilized.

Thus I came to write *The Time and Space of Uncle Albert* (Faber and Faber, 1989). It was a science fiction adventure story, except that the science was *fact* rather than fiction. It concerned a character named Uncle Albert (loosely modeled on Einstein) and his niece, Gedanken. I am happy to say it became an immediate bestseller and is now in fifteen translations. That book was quickly followed by others, including *Black Holes and Uncle Albert, Uncle Albert and the Quantum Quest, World of 1001 Mysteries,* and *Our Universe.*

Soon after my first children's book appeared, I attended a conference on science and religion. Also there was John Hull, professor of religious education at Birmingham University. During an interval between sessions, John took me to one side and said: "You know what you ought to be doing next, Russ. You should do for God what you have done for Einstein." When I asked what on earth he meant by that, he pointed out that survey research (in the United Kingdom) showed that around the age of eleven years, children begin to drift away from religion. This drift continues well into their late teens. In-depth research reveals that there are two main reasons for this hardening of attitudes: (1) an inability to come to terms with the problem of evil and suffering, i.e., why a good, all powerful God would allow bad things to happen; and (2) a perceived conflict between religion on the one hand, and what they were being newly taught in science lessons on the other. They were particularly disturbed by topics such as evolution by natural selection, Big Bang cosmology, and whether it was still possible to believe in miracles. John suggested that just as I was getting in quick with the ideas of Einstein before the children had become too fixed in erroneous ways of thinking about the world, so it was important to get in quick with ideas about the compatibility between religion and the modern scientific outlook, before the mistaken notion of an inevitable conflict took hold and led them to reject religion.

That was how I came to write *Here I Am!* (Faber and Faber, 1992), in which a child named Sam (who could be a Samuel or a Samantha—the reader is left to choose) has conversations through a computer with someone who claims to be God (but could equally be a human hacker—the reader again having to make up his or her own mind). The conversations range far and wide over science and religion, evil and suffering, etc. At the back of the book the reader is invited to ponder on some forty or so questions in the light of the information provided and the viewpoints expressed in the conversations.

My next major involvement with young people came with the making of the video series *The Question Is . . .* , which consists of four twenty-minute programs dealing with creation and cosmology, Genesis and evolution, miracles and the laws of nature, and the question of whether science provides the only route to knowledge. It was made in the BBC studios at the Open University with financing from the John Templeton Foundation. Without telling the children what they ought, or ought not, to believe, the series provides information on science, theology, and biblical criticism, together with a wide range of opposing viewpoints extending from atheism on the one hand to a variety of committed beliefs on the other. The intention is that the children are to reach their own conclusions—but conclusions that are well informed, rather than those they would otherwise be likely to draw based on muddled thinking and misconceptions about what science can and cannot say.

Throughout the making of the video series I worked in close contact with school teachers so as to ensure that it would fit into the ethos of school lessons and truly address the needs of the classroom situation. It was therefore gratifying to note that within fifteen months of the launch of the series at a press conference held at the Science Museum in London, thirty percent of all United Kingdom secondary schools had already bought a copy.

Though I have of late concentrated on the needs of children (because that is where I feel I can have maximum impact—whether in getting across straight science or the interplay between science and religion) I still continue to work with adults. This year I had a series entitled *Science and Wonders* go out on BBC Radio 4. It consisted of five forty-five minute programs of conversations with forty scientists, theologians, philosophers, and psychiatrists from both sides of the Atlantic. I discussed Freud's views on religion with a psychiatrist as together we sat on Freud's famous couch; I inquired of a biologist how Darwin's *Origin of Species* was first received as my interviewee sat in the chair where Darwin wrote that book; I explored with an artificial intelligence expert where her work was likely to lead as we listened to a computer improvising jazz in response to what it was hearing from human musicians. There were many, many fascinating conversations.

Science and Wonders was broadcast on the United Kingdom's most popular radio channel at prime listening time in the evening. It is not long ago that such a thing would have been unthinkable. Couple that with the extraordinary uptake of *The Question Is . . .* videos and we have a sure sign of the enormous interest that is now being generated in this subject area. I am delighted and exhilarated to think that my personal journey through religion should have led me into the thick of all this activity.

And yet I have to be careful not to get things out of proportion. There is a danger that the special nature of my distinctive ministry is likely to give rise in myself to an unbalanced spiritual life. So much of my time and effort is devoted to *arguing* about religion and the way it relates to other subjects such as physics, evolutionary biology, genetics, cosmology, psychology, and so on. But I am deeply aware that no one ever gets *argued* into a loving relationship with God—any more than one can expect to be argued into a loving relationship with one's future wife or husband. Getting to know and to love God is not like that. Arguing about religion can only ever be a first step, a means of clearing obstacles from one's path, obstacles to taking religion seriously. As such it clearly can have its uses. There are many people who would quite *like* to look into the claims of religion more deeply, but feel they cannot do so with intellectual integrity because of a mistaken belief that science has somehow disproved religion. If I am able to show that such reservations are groundless, thereby opening people up to the promptings of the spirit—making them receptive to a religion that can creep up on them in the way it crept up on me long ago—then I shall rest content.

10

PERSONAL REMINISCENCES

AND EXPECTATIONS

CARL FRIEDRICH VON WEIZSÄCKER

In which of my experiences did I myself encounter religion? How did I react?

I am descended from an Evangelical Lutheran family. My great-grandfather in the male line was a theologian. My mother taught me to pray with deep conviction. In my early childhood during the war we prayed to God that he protect my father and our relatives.

When I was twelve years old I began to read in the Bible and was deeply moved by the truth of the Sermon on the Mount. In my text on the course of politics I described this under the title "War and Peace." Thou shalt not kill. Love thine enemies. I intended, probably as a born natural scientist, to become an astronomer. But, as a result of my experiences, should I not have become a parson? Was it not now my life's task to preach this truth?

Many people of my generation, as a result of the natural sciences, lost their religious faith. Can one still believe in stories of miracles? Do not the stars in the skies run their course simply in accordance with the laws of mechanics? But my elementary feeling was the opposite even then. On a beautiful starry night in the Jura Mountains of Switzerland I perceived two certainties: here God is present; and the stars are spheres of gas, as physics teaches us today. God and the stars belong together, even though nobody had yet explained to me how they belong together. To find this out could be my life's task.

But why I could not become a parson of that time I learned a few years later. I sat at my school desk, a Protestant. Behind me a Roman Catholic, beside me a Jew. Several thousand kilometers away, the Moslems. Then the Hindus. Then the Buddhists. Had the all-benevolent God arranged to have me—of all people—born into the only true religion?

I never left the evangelical church into which I was born, but the question of how the truths of the religions relate to each other became central for me. Then, when I studied physics with Heisenberg in Leipzig, I attended a lecture by the distinguished and then still young religious historian, Joachim Wach, on the religions of Asia. I read the wonderful words of the Buddha in the translation by Karl Eugen Neumann, the writings of the Chinese with comments by Richard Wilhelm, and those of Lao-Tse, Confucius, and their successors. I read the Old Testament as a wise, magnificent source of early history.

But what are the experiences of a young and very inquisitive man in his church? The evangelical preaching services most likely strengthened my skepticism. The parson there was preaching in the solemn language that was then customary. Did he not know that what he was saying he did not really know? The Latin liturgy of the Catholic Church, with its two thousand years of religious experience, said more to me.

Things changed almost radically when Hitler came to power in 1933. On the one hand, his ardor initially appealed to a quasi-religious need in many of his young followers. On the other hand, the Christian church now had to defend the meaning of life. The "Bekennende Kirche" (Confessional Church) readopted early Christian practices. It prevailed, and, after the end of the Second World War, American Christians, especially Quakers, came to Germany and brought to the people suffering from hunger in the large cities food and love.

Thus my real view of worldwide Christianity opened itself. But, first, to come back to Germany. After the end of the war, there emerged a deep division between the western and the eastern states. In the Federal Republic, where I lived, the tradition of the Confessional Church was still alive and effective. On the other hand, the word

"Christian" became part of the name of the large conservative party, whose power was essentially middle class. In the D.D.R. (German Democratic Republic), the ruling party understood itself as socialist. I was in the D.D.R. every year since 1956, never as a guest of the government but always as a guest of the scientists and always also in close contact with the Evangelical and, at times, the Catholic Church. The fact that, in 1989–90, German reunification succeeded without bloodshed was to a large extent thanks to the church (in addition to the wisdom of Gorbachev). Experience in Hitler's Reich and in the D.D.R. has shown that the church was most effective where it was under political pressure. Today, after 1990, its effectiveness has rapidly declined.

Now, to the world. The topic "poverty and wealth" is the most visible here. Jesus again and again turned to the poor. Not that they should become rich, neither that they should starve; they should—and could—be open to each other and to God. During the decades of our century, the theology of liberation in South America was probably the largest attempt to follow this instruction.

My personal contacts were at first more in the political and social areas. The prevention of war was the initial topic of the Max-Planck-Institut zur Erforschung der Lebensbedingungen der wissenschaftlich-technischen Welt (Max Planck Institute for Research into Living Conditions in the Scientific and Technological World). On worldwide social matters, I was given practical information by the Deutscher Entwicklungsdienst (German Development Service), which sent young aid workers to many countries, and on whose behalf I visited India, parts of Africa, and once Central America. I was involved in Christian work by the Oekumenischer Rat der Kirchen (Ecumenical Council of Churches) in Geneva. It organized the Konziliarer Prozess für Gerechtigkeit, Frieden und Bewahrung der Schöpfung (Conciliar Process for Justice, Peace and Preservation of Creation) in 1983–1990, initially suggested in a proposal for a council of peace by representatives of the Evangelical Church in the D.D.R. I participated in the conferences in Basle in 1989 and in Seoul, Korea, in 1990 on behalf of the Evangelical Church. I was also a guest at the Day of Prayer for Peace of the World's Religions convened by the pope in 1986 in Assisi. Eventually I obtained contact in writing with the Chicago Parliament of World Religions in 1993, a repetition of an 1893 assembly by the same name and at the same location with the goal of a "World Ethic."

Were these gatherings successful? There intellectual representatives of the religious communities expressed demands on the future that I consider vital. But resonance among the public was, given the progressing decline of influence of the religions, only slight.

I will attempt to say what would be important to me in the three areas of ethics, inner experience, and theology. The quest for a common ethic, be it formulated in religious or secular terms, seems imperative to me for peace, social justice, and the protection of nature. That was my concern from the beginning.

But then, in my encounter with the religions, meditative experience became one of the most important steps on the path. I had probably already been prepared for it in my childhood. I perceived some of it in Catholic liturgy. From an evangelical viewpoint, I experienced it as a guest of the Michaelsbruderschaft (Brotherhood of St. Michael). But the deepest experience I had much later, during my first visit to India, at the grave of the Hindu holy man, Ramana Maharshi. Hindus and Buddhists may take this kind of experience for granted, but I found it to be unusual and deeply moving. Among these, meetings I had in Japan were educational, and then so were my increasingly important contacts with the Dalai Lama.

Theology, finally, is the attempt to express rationally what is being experienced and sought. This rationality inevitably led me to science and philosophy.

ABOUT THE AUTHORS

AND EDITORS

Charles Birch is a professor emeritus of the University of Sydney, Australia, and has held posts in ecology and genetics at Chicago, Oxford, Columbia, Sao Paulo, Minnesota, and California. He was awarded the Templeton Prize for Progress in Religion in 1990.

S. Jocelyn Bell Burnell is a professor of physics at the Open University in England and chairs that department. She is also presiding clerk of the Society of Friends (Quakers) in Britain (i.e., England, Scotland, and Wales). An astronomer, she is one of the discoverers of pulsars.

Larry Dossey, a physician of internal medicine, is former chief of staff of Medical City Dallas (Texas) Hospital and former co-chair of the Panel on Mind/Body Interventions, Office of Complementary and Alternative Medicine, National Institutes of Health (U.S.A.).

Owen Gingerich is a professor of astronomy and the history of science at the Harvard-Smithsonian Center for Astrophysics, Cambridge, Massachusetts.

Kenneth Seeman Giniger heads a New York publishing company and is chairman emeritus of the Layman's National Bible Association.

Peter E. Hodgson heads the Nuclear Physics Theoretical Group, Nuclear Physics Laboratory, Oxford University, and is a fellow of Corpus Christi College.

Stanley L. Jaki is a Benedictine priest and professor of history and philosophy of science at Seton Hall University, U.S.A. He was awarded the Templeton Prize for Progress in Religion in 1987.

Arthur Peacocke, whose primary scientific discipline was physical biochemistry, is director of the Ian Ramsey Centre, Oxford University; warden emeritus of the Society of Ordained Scientists; and honorary canon of Christ Church Cathedral, Oxford, England.

John Polkinghorne recently retired as president of Queens' College, Cambridge, and was knighted by the Her Majesty Queen Elizabeth II. Formerly professor of mathematical physics at Cambridge, he is a priest, a former member of the Church of England Doctrine Committee, and a member of General Synod.

Russell Stannard is the former vice president of the Institute of Physics and professor of physics at the Open University, England. He has served on the Prime Minister's Advisory Committee on Science and Technology in the United Kingdom.

John Marks Templeton founded the Templeton group of investment mutual funds and, since his retirement from investment management, has devoted his efforts to writing and philanthropic activities such as the Templeton Prize for Progress in Religion and the Templeton foundations. He was knighted by Her Majesty Queen Elizabeth II in 1987.

Carl Friedrich von Weizsäcker, physicist and philosopher, is a professor at the Max-Planck-Gesellschaft in Germany. He was awarded the Templeton Prize for Progress in Religion in 1989.